A
Clergy, Re __ __, *and* **Wholeness**

"In *Clergy, Retirement, and Wholeness*, Dr. Halaas provides a thought-provoking guide to living well up to and through retirement. While her focus is on clergy and their spouses, it provides information and encouragement that everyone can use. A comprehensive and inspirational guide for clergy and their families as well as for church groups who want to support health in all aspects of life."

—Barbara A. Boigegrain
United Methodist Church General Board
of Pension and Health Benefits

"Don't be mistaken, this book is not about retirement—not if you think retirement lies far in the future. This book is about seizing this moment and living life abundantly. Most clergy spend their life helping others through life's difficulties. Often, that means reminding people of the need to balance work and recreation, and spending time with family. It's a message clergy themselves can forget. With clear, warm, sensitive persuasion, Gwen Halaas, a physician and a minister's spouse, puts the gift of work in its proper place: balance and wholeness are essential to the ordained minister's vocation."

—Rev. Canon Dawn Davis
Anglican Diocese of Toronto

"The health of clergy has been declining steadily over the past decade. What are the causes and how can we stop this trend? This book, written by a family physician, is specifically for clergy who want to enhance their health and wellness in mid-life as they look forward to retirement. It addresses six aspects of health: physical, emotional, intellectual, social, vocational, and spiritual. Easy to read and packed full of important information, every clergy person should read this book—and then do what Halaas advises!"

—Harold G. Koenig, M.D.
Duke University Medical Center

Clergy, Retirement, and Wholeness

Looking Forward to the Third Age

Gwen Wagstrom Halaas

THE
ALBAN
INSTITUTE

www.alban.org

Scripture quotations, unless otherwise noted, are from the New Revised Standard Version of the Bible, copyright © 1989, Division of Christian Education of the National Council of the Churches of Christ in the United States of America and are used by permission.

The Wholeness Wheel on page 5 is used with the permission of the InterLutheran Coordinating Committee on Ministerial Health and Wellness of the Evangelical Lutheran Church in America and the Lutheran Church–Missouri Synod. Copyright © 1997-2004.

The food pyramid on page 24 is reprinted with the permission of Simon & Schuster Adult Publishing Group from *Eat, Drink, and Be Healthy: The Harvard Medical School Guide to Healthy Eating* by Walter C. Willett, M.D. Copyright © 2001 by President and Fellows of Harvard College.

Cover design by Adele Robey, Phoenix Graphics.

Library of Congress Cataloging-in-Publication Data

Halaas, Gwen Wagstrom, 1954-
  Clergy, retirement, and wholeness : looking forward to the third age / Gwen Wagstrom Halaas.
    p. cm.
  Includes bibliographical references.
  ISBN 1-56699-300-8
  1. Clergy—Retirement. I. Title.

BV4382.H35 2005
253'.2—dc22   2005009324

09 08 07 06 05   VG   1 2 3 4 5

Contents

Foreword

For ministers considering retirement, wouldn't it be wonderful to have the opportunity to sit down for a few hours with a competent and caring and faithful family physician to chat about what lies ahead—and how to stay healthy and happy in body and spirit? In this book, family physician Gwen Wagstrom Halaas gives us that opportunity!

To help leaders (and their families) faithfully look forward and prepare not just to survive, but to thrive, in retirement Dr. Halaas expands her acclaimed work on ministerial health and wellness by focusing on the realistic vulnerabilities and special possibilities of retirement.

Challenging the concept of clergy retirement as an ending or withdrawal, Dr. Halaas refers to retirement as "the Third Age." She defines the Third Age as "potentially the most important and rewarding time of life" and an opportunity "to use [our] life experiences to enrich the lives of others."

Dr. Halaas perceives retirement as an inviting series of "R's," such as reappraisal, reaffirmation, reallocation, reawakening, rekindling, renewal, and rediscovery. And these are only some of the opportunities of retirement when retirement is recognized as a time of "recommitting to the service of God."

What can get in the way of our realizing all the potential of retirement? As she did in *The Right Road: Life Choices for Clergy*, Dr. Halaas uses her experience as a physician to identify, diagnose, and prescribe a path to clergy health and wholeness, but this time she identifies issues with particular relevance for the retirement years. As the wife of a parish pastor, and as a caregiver knowledgeable about the demands of ministry on seminarians and ministers and their spouses, Dr. Halaas speaks with empathetic understanding as well as medical competence. This combination of competence and caring pervades her writing and is a special gift to ministers and their families, but makes insightful reading for pastor-parish and mutual ministry committees as well.

Twenty years ago, in *Pastor As Person* and *The Faith-hardy Christian*, I reported the research results after thousands of administrations of my holistic Faith-hardiness Inventory. When asked to put in rank order the physical (body), mental (thinking), emotional (feeling), social (relating), and spiritual (believing), clergy consistently ranked the physical lowest. This pattern is consistent with present studies on ministerial health and wellness, and here is where Dr. Halaas makes a remarkable contribution in her chapter on health and wellness in midlife and her chapter on "Let's Get Real: Physical Health." For those of us who may conclude that it is too late or that there is nothing we can do to improve our health, Dr. Halaas shares the good news that "the majority of factors that impact our health...are our lifestyle behaviors...(and) these are factors we can control."

With relevant and challenging questions at the end of each chapter, Dr. Halaas follows her discussion of physical health issues with chapters on emotional, intellectual, social, vocational, and spiritual health. "Where's the joy?" is a question which leads into a presentation of a different kind of intelligence, emotional intelligence, and how to attain it.

In contrast to conceptions that focus on the intellectual losses of aging, Dr. Halaas points to the resilience of the aging brain, the "advantages that form the basis for wisdom," and the brain's "capacity to grow—not physically, but in usefulness." A particularly interesting linkage is made between intellectual health and listening to or performing music.

Maintaining social and vocational health are difficult challenges during active ministry. In chapters 5 and 6, Dr. Halaas deals directly with the implications of what is true for many clergy: "identity and social function is entirely defined by [our] occupation...[which leaves a] gaping hole in retirement." She demonstrates her experience and understanding of the open-endedness of ministry and how "passion without boundaries or without balance can become fatal—physically or vocationally." Here, as in the other chapters, Dr. Halaas follows keen diagnosis with creative prescriptions for wholeness and health.

"While we may have retired from our occupation, we have vocations until the end. Sharing our gifts and talents and the love of God with others continues to give us a sense of purpose." In her chapters on faith and life, and dying well, Dr. Halaas shows how a robust spirituality undergirds wholeness and, as current research is increasingly substantiating, impacts health. As spirituality underlies living life to the fullest, so spiritual health makes it possible for us to live faithfully into the end of life—and Dr. Halaas suggests practical ways to care for those we will leave behind.

The Alban Institute has a long-standing commitment both to ministry and to persons in ministry. While in the parish, when teaching in the seminary, and while serving as a synodical staff person, I have looked to Alban time and time again for leading edge publications. As one who has researched and written about ministerial health and wellness for over thirty years, I have high expectations when I read the work of others. Dr. Halaas meets and exceeds those high expectations not only by confirming previous studies but also by adding a distinctive new dimension by virtue of her professional expertise and interdisciplinary sensitivities. There are those who say that the best teachers help us come to understand what we already know, which Dr. Halaas does, but in this book she also has taught me to look at retirement in new ways. As you begin your conversation with Dr. Halaas in this book, listen both for confirmation and challenge. If you do, I believe you will learn as I did that, in the Third Age, the best may be yet to come!

Rev. Dr. Gary L. Harbaugh
Professor Emeritus of Pastoral Care and Psychology
Trinity Lutheran Seminary, Columbus, Ohio

Preface

What would you wish for in retirement? Good health and enough financial stability not to have to worry about your daily needs? A healthy, loving partner or other family or friends with the time and the desire to enjoy activities with you? A supportive social community in your neighborhood or church that gives you opportunities to be engaged in life and to continue to learn? Opportunities to travel, to meet new people and to learn new things?

Health is essential if we want to pursue opportunities, to make choices freely, and to enjoy the autumn years of life. If our physical or mental health declines to the point that it requires most of our energy to manage the activities of daily living, we cannot live life to our full potential because our spiritual, intellectual, vocational, and social health are affected as well. If our health is poor, we need others' help, their time and energy. Retiring well is everyone's goal, but accomplishing this end requires planning and effort.

I am a family physician who has spent years working with patients to improve their health and wellness and teaching young physicians how to care for patients. Early in my professional career, it became apparent that physicians are not good at practicing self-care. As the wife of a pastor, I recognized the same vulnerability in those engaged in public ministry. Professional caregivers are not good role models for health and wellness. The result of failing to practice self-care can be physical illness, mental illness, loss of relationships, loss of joy in work, and uncaring, transaction-based relationships with others. If your professional and personal life is consumed by the needs of others, it is difficult to have a satisfactory personal life. You risk burning out physically or mentally or becoming vulnerable to unhealthy relationships within the work world. Just as physicians may use medical language or a white coat as a professional barrier to protect themselves emotionally, so pastors may erect walls to protect themselves from being consumed by need; they may become distant from their parishioners and co-workers and often from their families.

Staying vital and healthy as a professional caregiver requires good habits of self-care. This aim means knowing our strengths and weaknesses, our gifts and our challenges—physically, emotionally, intellectually, socially, vocationally, and spiritually. It means taking the time daily, weekly, and periodically to be renewed and re-energized. It means building up our reserves to call upon in difficult times. It means continuing to grow and change to keep up with the changes around us.

Good health and self-care are particularly important in changing times. Change will continue, and at a more rapid pace. Today's retirees grew up expecting to prepare for a single lifelong career or a single role within the home; they thought of retirement as a time for rest and recreation. Baby boomers were raised with the idea that they would experience several jobs during their lifetime and began to think about retirement as a time for experiences they had postponed—travel, education, time with grandchildren. Now we know that it is not unusual to have several careers within a lifetime and that we may expect to continue to work in some fashion long beyond "retirement age" for financial and other reasons.

This book is a guide to health and wellness, written specifically for clergy and church workers but relevant to all who are considering retirement in their future. The chapters address various dimensions of health—physical, emotional, intellectual, social/interpersonal, vocational, and spiritual. The stories reflect the realities of the ongoing journey toward health and wellness; they are fictional, although some of the details reflect the lives of real individuals. I hope that you will find this book informative, inspirational, and encouraging. We have much to give to others, to the church and to the world. The energy to create, work, worship, and serve comes from good health.

Acknowledgments

As one who dreams about retirement and is in the planning stage, I have found the writing of this book a meaningful labor. I am most thankful for my partner in life and in retirement planning, my best friend and husband, Mark. We are thankful for the healthful and loving examples our parents have provided. This book would not be what it is without the helpful and diligent editing of Beth Gaede. And my understanding and love for the church and its people have grown immeasurably through many conversations with pastors and lay leaders throughout the Evangelical Lutheran Church in America as they have shared their stories of ministry and life.

Prologue

The 25 years since we graduated from seminary have gone by in the blink of an eye, and our lives have changed immeasurably. A few of us look just the same, several look like their parents, and most of us look familiar but softer, rounder, slightly out of focus. About three-fourths of the class members have returned for a reunion. We know that one classmate, Paul, died of cancer in his 30s. Rumors had circulated about other classmates' problems, some medical. We are all looking for an opportunity to reconnect. Some are seeking reassurance that their comfortable but unexciting lives have had meaning; others are eager to share accomplishments and opinions.

I scan the room to see who is here. Before I see him, I hear Jim. He has always been the life of the party—if you don't hear his distinct voice, you can find him in the midst of raucous laughter. His wife, Judy, is at his side, as always, radiating the joy of a happy life. In the laughing crowd I also spot George—a party lover, but one whose job is always to encourage the antics of Jim. In another corner I see Michael, expounding on some theological insight to an admiring crowd. The brightest one in the class, Michael is also a very gentle creature, beloved by his congregation of the past 12 years.

I hear the happy exclamations as Ellen and Jean find each other. Fast friends in seminary, they were as different as night and day. Jean came to seminary after 10 years of teaching in the elementary grades while raising her children. With the children grown and on their own, she divorced after seminary and began her ministry in a two-point rural call. Ellen came to seminary straight from college, started her ministry as an associate in a large congregation, and is now senior pastor of another large congregation. She is married and has three children.

I am not a pastor. I am a family physician and the wife of a pastor. These are my husband's seminary classmates. Although he always knew he would be a pastor, he was also a latecomer to seminary. We had decided that I would finish medical school first while he earned a living. As children came into our family, we were able to integrate education, training, and our professional lives. My husband is the main reason for our success. He is a marvelous father and a gifted minister. Our lives, like everyone else's here, have been busy and satisfying. Anticipating and returning to be together face-to-face is more than reminiscing and catching up. It is recapturing those years of being students together. That was a time of fun, learning, and growth. It was also a special time of claiming one's call and vocation, preparing for and anticipating the future. We are here today celebrating the simple joy of being together, reconnecting, and perhaps renewing the passion for public ministry.

It doesn't take long. We recognize one another and reconnect—telling stories of times remembered and experiences after seminary. We laugh and cry, mostly tears of happiness. Many have raised children and have been in and out of two or three congregations. Some have lost parents or are making time to care for ailing parents. Eventually the conversation turns: "So now, what's next for you?" Many of us share professional and personal goals. Some are already making retirement plans—considering financial readiness and researching desirable locations. We hear reactions of surprise to the retirement discussion and wisecracks about getting old. Most of us are slightly envious that our peers would be so organized or have the foresight to plan for a successful retirement. Most of us are feeling dizzy from the merry-go-round of marriage-children-careers-plus. Planning for life after the merry-go-round is a novelty. We have been trying for so many years just to avoid falling off.

1

It's All about Change
Health and Wellness in Midlife

The word "midlife" is often paired with "crisis." In North America, in this era of relative good health, midlife is four or five decades long. Let's hope our midlife is not one big crisis. This book is a guide to using the accomplishments and the transitions of midlife to plan for living well in retirement. If we approach this time as an opportunity for periodic reflection—of lessons learned, skills developed, choices made, and accomplishments—and if we begin to set goals and to continue our learning while looking forward to and planning for retirement, we will have reason to hope that we can avoid that stereotypical crisis.

A midlife crisis is all about change. Our bodies and our looks change. Children grow up and move away. Relationships shift. Parents get sick or die. Jobs alter. Communities change. The skills we learn, the habits we develop, the knowledge we gain cannot carry us through a lifetime. The typical midlife crisis is an effort to take control of changes that have gone beyond our control. If we anticipate change and remain flexible and adaptable, we can avoid the defensive reactions of meeting change head-on.

Most of us simply react to change as it happens. This book is about planning for change. Becoming a pastor required years—discernment, seminary, internship, first call or appointment. Public ministry as a pastor occupies that middle third of life. Surely the final third, at a time when you have developed many skills, know your strengths and gifts, and have the wisdom gained from the experience of the first two-thirds of life deserves a similar investment of time and energy to plan and prepare.

Health and Wellness

Being healthy involves being flexible and adaptable. It doesn't mean being in perfect physical shape; rather, it means being in balance and doing our best daily to meet our physical, emotional, social, intellectual, vocational, and spiritual needs.

The Institute of Medicine, one of the National Academies of Science created by Congress to advance and disseminate scientific knowledge about human health, has published a report on health and behavior that defines the qualities of positive health:

1. a healthy body,
2. high-quality personal relationships,
3. a sense of purpose in life,
4. self-regarded mastery of life's tasks, and
5. resilience to stress, trauma, and change.[1]

What do we know about positive health in midlife that we did not know as young adults? We are, one hopes, no longer taking a healthy body for granted. We have likely experienced a significant illness or injury that has made us aware of vulnerability and limitation. We have also had positive experiences with physical success—athletic prowess, mastery of physical skills, improvement in our level of fitness, or achievement of a healthy weight. We are beginning to face the reality of a limited lifespan. We are recognizing that the better we started out and the more effort we have exerted along the way, the better physical quality of life we may have as we begin an inevitable decline over time.

We have learned much about relationships. We have likely had a significant intimate relationship that has tested our ability to share and to compromise. It has probably given us an opportunity to experience the absolute highs and absolute lows emotionally. It has enabled us to learn more about ourselves as reflected in our partner's eyes. We may have had children—learning again the depth of love and the heights of frustration. We have had to learn patience and have experienced joy in observing milestones achieved. Relationships have enabled us to learn more about our own idiosyncrasies, gifts, and limitations.

We are discovering more about our own purpose in life. Even if we have been working toward occupational or family goals from a young age, we are beginning to see the impact of our choices and to have more control over our accomplishments. At midlife we begin to reflect from the vantage point of a life rich with experience, a life that is probably past its midpoint. The ripple effects of our decisions and life experiences have resulted in a sphere of influence within which our purpose becomes clearer. Rather than claiming individual goals of achievement or attainment, we begin to look at the impact on others of the work we do.

Midlife is a time to recognize our mastery of life's tasks: a fulfilling marriage, happy children, completion of educational degrees, vocational success, recognition for work well done. It is also a time when we recognize certain skills we have not mastered, and decide to accept or to address that lack of mastery.

Positive health means developing resilience to stress, trauma, or change. Having lived through five or six decades, we have inevitably been exposed to stress, trauma, and change. We have known failure and achieved success, suffered and grown, learned and refused to learn—or retreated into denial. Midlife is also critical because that resiliency will be challenged in ways that are new or more intense. Whether by the death of a loved one, a personal health crisis, the loss of a job, or a significant challenge with a child or relative, we are likely to face challenges in midlife.

Being healthy means attending to all aspects of health and wellness in a proactive and habitual way. A wonderfully helpful picture of this model of health was developed by the InterLutheran Coordinating Committee on Ministerial Health and Wellness—a committee of pastors, teachers, church leaders (including bishops, district presidents, and administrative leaders), and members of the pension and health plans of the Evangelical Lutheran Church in America and the Lutheran Church–Missouri Synod.

In this picture, at right, you are at the center. As a baptized individual you are a new creation in Christ and a member of the body of Christ. Living well is the result of balancing all areas of health, from physical well-being to intellectual well-being. For the faithful, these areas of health are surrounded by and supported by our spiritual health.

Because of our life experiences, the picture presented by the Wholeness Wheel is meaningful. Midlife, or the third age, is to reflect on our baptism and what it means to be a new creation in Christ. Baptism and newness may seem somewhat distant, but our understanding of baptism's sacramental nature and the importance of being a member of the body of Christ is more clear. By this time, we have experienced the fullness of life and the fullness of God's love and grace. We understand better because of life experience what it means to be a member of the body of Christ. We know what it means to be a member of a family or a congregation, to be a member of a team contributing different functions, skills and gifts.

Self-care

As members of the body of Christ, we must do our best. The body functions fully as a result of the coordinated effort and function of all members. If part of the body is not functioning

Wholeness Wheel

---

optimally, it falls on the other members or organs to take up the slack. When you rely on a body part for your vocation, caring for it is a priority. Singers care for their voices, pianists their hands, and quarterbacks their arms. What is any single body part without the whole?

Self-care is essential to being healthy. Some confuse self-care with selfishness and think that taking the time to tend to oneself is time unfairly taken from attending to the needs of others. Taking responsibility for one's own health is a sign of maturity and wisdom. In midlife we know ourselves well—our strengths and weaknesses, our state of health, our state of mind. Having knowledge and familiarity with our state of health is not enough. Practicing self-care is being aware of your needs and relationships with others. It is nurturing your physical, emotional, intellectual, social/interpersonal, vocational, and spiritual health so that you can be of service to others.

The needs of babies are straightforward—nourishment, comfort, rest, and social activity or contact. They have limited ways to help themselves, however, and must ask for help by making noise. For adults, the basic needs remain the same—nourishment, comfort, rest, and social contact. Satisfying these needs becomes more complex for us as individuals, though, because we have developed the ability to take care of ourselves and have the responsibility of making decisions about how to meet these needs.

We can decide to eat three meals and healthy snacks every day, or we can choose to consume doughnuts and coffee and fast food. We can get eight hours of sleep most nights—or three hours. We can be social animals or totally reclusive. We can be physically active or couch potatoes. We can live lives faithful to God, or give in to every human desire.

Again, middle age gives us handy reminders about the importance of self-care. We don't function well without sleep or without breakfast, lunch, and dinner. If we sit too long, we stiffen up and have to move around. Our bodies give us signs; we have to learn to be attentive. We should eat when we are hungry, sleep when we are tired, get up and move about when we are restless. Sometimes we shouldn't wait for signs. We should drink water regularly—thirst is a signal that you have already fallen behind the necessary quantity of water your body needs over the course of the day. The same is true for urinating. Don't wait for the signs, do it when you have the chance.

We are our own caretakers, but we also have important relationships. We can eat for convenience and pleasure, or we can share meals with family or friends. We can "party hearty" and suffer at work or in our relationships with family. We can work at a job that simply pays the bills, or we can search for a meaningful vocation that satisfies our own needs and the needs of others.

We need energy and clear minds to know ourselves and to make good decisions about our lives. Nothing is more precious than a satisfied and happy baby cooing and gurgling; likewise, nothing is more frustrating or distressing than hearing the cries of a baby who is tired, hungry, or in need of attention. We need to care for ourselves by meeting the basic needs of nourishment, comfort, rest and social activity or contact. Our bodies and minds need to be fed healthy food at regular intervals. They need consistent and adequate rest to function fully. They need to be stimulated by regular physical activity. We need intimate social relationships to better understand ourselves and to be happy. We need to be fulfilled in our vocation by using our talents to make the world a better place. We need to have a relationship with God to help us lead fulfilling lives.

In *Let Your Life Speak*, Parker Palmer, educator and author, writes: "Self-care is never a selfish act—it is simply good stewardship of the only gift I have, the gift I was put on earth to offer to others. Anytime we can listen to true self and give it the care it requires, we do so not only for ourselves but for the many others whose lives we touch."[2]

Self-care is not something that can be done as a prescription—to rescue one from the ravages of life. Self-care is an expression of self-love that should be a lifelong habit. Those who establish the habits of good self-care from an early age will maximize their health and vitality. They will be in balance—able to feel fulfilled and yet ready for continued growth and change. Self-care gets us through the times of life that are challenging. During the years of raising young children and adolescents, difficulty with relationships or the pain of divorce, career change or job loss, diagnosis of a chronic disease, or loss of full bodily function through illness or injury—through all these challenges, self-care ensures a strong foundation that will soften their impact.

We never outgrow our need for self-care; we will always benefit from it. Practicing self-care is a means to a meaningful and healthy retirement—a major life change for those who have had lengthy careers and for those whose partners have been working outside the home. Maximizing physical, emotional, intellectual, vocational, and spiritual health creates readiness for the changes encountered in retirement.

What Is Retirement?

How many times have you heard the words, "When I retire..."? Were the words that followed inspiring? Did those words reflect a well-thought-out plan? Or were they generic, oversimplified, or meaningless phrases? Like: "I'm going fishing." "I'm going to travel." "I'm going to do just what I want to do." Or "I'm going to do all those things I've been wanting to do for years." Sometimes the words express doubt, or even fear. "What will I do when I retire? What will happen to me?"

One of my patients would tell me at each medical visit how many years, months, and days she had left until retirement. She came to see me shortly after her retirement, looking younger and refreshed and expressing excitement about the time she was going to spend with her husband, grandchildren and children, and friends. Several months later she returned in tears. She had concerns about her husband's health. She loved being with her children and grandchildren but felt overwhelmed at times with being needed. And when she went out with friends, she found her husband becoming more and more jealous and suspicious. What had been a dream for years was turning into a nightmare.

For those of us who have the luxury of anticipating retirement, counting down the days is not adequate preparation. One may feel an immediate relief upon dropping the burdens and frustrations of daily work and a joy and freedom in living without a time schedule. Within days or weeks, however, a new reality sets in. Relationships change, habits change, and physical health may change dramatically. Pre-existing problems may become more apparent, and adjusting to this new reality may not be easy. Time management is as important in retirement as it was on the job or during the years of raising children. Patterns of communication with a spouse who worked in the past are sometimes jarringly inadequate in retirement. For some, retirement is unplanned, sudden, and traumatic, coming as the result of personal injury or illness or the illness of a loved one.

"Retirement" is defined by *Merriam-Webster's Online Dictionary* as "withdrawal from one's position or occupation or from active working life," or "the act of removal, vacating, separation."[3] It is synonymous with reclusion or seclusion. In the past, one may have retired in declining health with only a few years of life remaining. Today many retire with decades of life ahead, potentially one-third of one's lifespan. We need to take a fresh look at the concept of retirement and to get away from the dictionary definition of withdrawal from active working life, just as we must not view health as the absence of disease. The work of the first third of life is to mature as a human being. The work of the second third of life is to experience life and to learn from those experiences in preparation for the third age.

Joe retired from parish ministry at age 69. He spent the first month rearranging his home office with the books and resources he had brought home from the church office. He had attended several retirement parties in his honor with family, friends, and members of the congregation. His wife, Patsy, had retired from teaching several years earlier. Her days were busy as she did volunteer work for the church's program for the homeless and the community food shelf. She had her Bible study group, the church choir, and her quilting group. She went to the health club twice a week for water aerobics. She was happy and was looking forward to seeing more of her husband.

Joe and Patsy continued to attend the church where he had been senior pastor. Joe was comfortable sitting in the back pew at the early service, but he didn't feel comfortable getting involved in other congregational ministries. It was like "going back to work," and he was afraid of stepping on the new senior pastor's toes. The physical move from the church office to home had tired him out, and he was noticing more aches and pains. He would often nap during the day when Patsy was away, and then find that he didn't sleep well at night. By the end of the second month, the bishop called. A small congregation was in desperate need of an interim minister because of the current pastor's sudden health problems. Joe jumped at the chance to be useful again, although he wondered if he had the energy.

The work of the third age of life is to use your life experiences to enrich the lives of others. It is potentially the most important and most rewarding time of life. In place of "retire," let's consider some other words: reactivate, reaffirm, reallocate, reappraise, reawaken, recommission, reconfigure, reconsecrate, recontextualize, rededicate, rediscover, reevaluate, reinspire, rekindle, renew. Let's use more active and inclusive words for this third life change. It is a time to rekindle the flame of youthful passion with the wisdom of life's experiences. It is a rebaptism, or a reaffirmation of what it means to be a child of God. It may be a rechanneling of energy in a new direction—it may be directed outward toward others or inward to meet personal needs. It may be the opportunity for recommissioning in terms of recognizing the gift of grace and recommitting yourself to the service of God.

Jean retired from parish ministry at age 66. She had taken a sabbatical four years earlier, after 12 years of ministry in the congregation she was serving—seven years as senior pastor. During her sabbatical she had taken a photography class at the local community college. Photography had been her passion in college, where she had minored in art and directed photography for the yearbook. She put away her camera when she went to seminary, and other than the photos she had taken of her growing family, she hadn't given photography another thought. Jean loved her sabbatical time, learning more about photographic techniques and photo development. She created a portfolio of nature photos of which she was proud, and which were a source of inspiration to her in her final years of ministry. She had also taken yoga classes during her sabbatical and had created a daily routine. As a result, she was more limber than she had been in years and found the practice stress-relieving and energizing.

Jean and her husband had grown apart after 20 years of marriage and had divorced 14 years earlier. She was proud of her adult children and pleased to be a mentor to her youngest son, who was now in seminary. Jean was excited about retiring. She had set up a darkroom in her basement and had enrolled in a photography seminar at Yosemite National Park. She was considering applying for an art photography fellowship at a retreat center in Santa Fe. Two years earlier, Jean had moved from her family home to a condominium and was pleased to not have the hassle of keeping up a house and lawn as she was making new plans. Jean loved the theater and had season tickets this year with her closest friend. She looked forward to having that time to catch up and enjoy a mutual interest. She had just joined a photography club through the community college's adult senior education hostel program. It was an opportunity to meet new friends and to share ideas. Jean had recently met a man who was becoming a good friend, and she was looking forward to having the time and freedom to see if the friendship would develop into a more intimate relationship.

Do you recognize these stories? Joe and Jean have different approaches to retirement. What will life be like for Jean and Joe in five or 10 years? What will your life be like after you retire from your life's work? Have you thought about it? Have you made plans? Have you made changes in your life to pave the way for success in your new way of living? Have you already retired? In America, many of us will have 20 or more years of retirement. Think about your professional or working life. Have you made plans over the years? Have they been annual plans, five-year plans, 10-year plans? Have you made plans that involved your financial well-being? Have you prepared for a possible loss of job, onset of illness, or disability? Have you planned regular vacations, family or school reunions, or continued education? Why should you approach 20 years of "retirement" any differently?

Living well in retirement encompasses health, joy, growth, purpose, and relationships with others and with God. Let's explore the issues in facts and fiction that will help in reflecting and planning for retirement rather than just dreaming about it.

For Reflection

1. When do you plan to retire? What steps are you taking to prepare for retirement?
2. What significant changes do you anticipate as a result of retiring from work?
3. Describe your current state of health. Describe your health in terms of the Wholeness Wheel on page 5.
4. What is your vision for a happy retirement?
5. What is your passion in life?

6. What have you been unable to do while working that you look forward to doing in retirement?
7. In what areas would you like to continue to grow and learn in retirement?
8. What expertise do you bring to others in your retirement?

2

Let's Get Real
Physical Health

In a recent study of pastors in the Evangelical Lutheran Church in America (average age: 50), two out of three were overweight, one in three was obese, one in four had high blood pressure and high cholesterol, and nearly one in five had suffered from serious depression in the past year.[1] These statistics should be seen in the context of a growing concern about weight, heart disease, diabetes, and depression in America. These health issues appear to have a higher incidence in pastors than in the general population, however, and the implications of these health problems are significant for those in public ministry with its demands and public exposure. The health of church leaders affects the health and vitality of congregations and ultimately the church at large.

From a personal perspective, the toll is significant. Being overweight, stressed, depressed, or living with a chronic condition such as heart disease or diabetes saps energy and leaves little time and energy for family or friends, vocational growth, innovation, or change. From the Wholeness Wheel perspective (see page 5), it's like driving on a flat tire. You are more prone to accidents and not likely to get very far, very fast. The best approach is to pull over out of traffic and fix the flat, even if it is a temporary fix. If you continue to drive on a tire with low air pressure, the sidewalls of the tire will begin to break down, and the tire or rim will ultimately be ruined.

These health issues and the resulting vulnerability are primarily the result of our lifestyle behaviors. The effect is cumulative over decades. The reality of the physical toll is experienced in our 30s and 40s. The sooner we address lifestyles and habits, the better. The good news is that lifestyle changes do make a difference. In a recent study, individuals who lost from 5 percent to 7 percent of their weight decreased their risk for diabetes by 58 percent.[2] It's important to accept that we do have control over our physical health. Although other factors influence how long and how well we live—genetics, medical errors, or exposure to toxins, for example—our lifestyle behaviors are primarily responsible for early death or illness.

Health Issues of Midlife

We are familiar with the top medical causes of death in America. In 2002 for people ages 45 to 64, they were cancer, heart disease, accidental injuries, stroke, diabetes, and chronic respiratory diseases. There is some good news: the number of deaths due to heart disease and stroke has declined over the past 50 years. But deaths from cancer have stayed steady. Over age 65 heart disease is number one, followed by cancer, stroke, chronic respiratory disease, influenza and pneumonia, and Alzheimer's disease.[3]

In the United States in 2002, the *actual* causes of death (not the diseases themselves, but the behaviors or exposures that resulted in death or fatal diseases) were tobacco use, poor diet, physical inactivity, alcohol consumption, bacteria or viruses causing such infections as influenza and pneumonia, toxic agents such as pollutants and asbestos, motor vehicles, firearms, unprotected sexual behavior, and the use of illicit drugs. The top two causes, tobacco use and obesity, are almost equally dangerous, and each accounts for about one in five deaths per year compared to less than 2 percent of deaths each due to motor vehicle accidents, discharge of firearms, risky sexual behavior, and use of illicit drugs.[4]

Physical inactivity and obesity are intimately related, and both significantly increase our risk for many diseases. Many of us see the light at the first mention of a serious health problem from our physician: "Your blood pressure [blood sugar, cholesterol] is running a bit high. I think we need to get serious about some changes to avoid medication." By that time we have had decades to establish our habits: running off to work without breakfast; drinking several cups of coffee to get started; picking up a drive-through lunch; eating a big, late dinner; sitting through evening meetings or mindless television; falling asleep; and then getting up to go to bed.

To complicate matters, although heart disease is predicted to continue as the number-one cause of death and chronic illness, depression is predicted to rise to number two. If you think changing your habits is tough, try doing it when you're depressed. The good news here is physical activity. It's the place to start because it increases energy and improves your mood. The time to do it is sooner rather than later. Physicians know that patients do listen to their advice and make changes—especially when they have had to break some bad news. The diagnosis of a medical problem offers a timely opportunity to influence behavior change, but one that could be avoided. Each of us can improve our health by making small changes in our lifestyle. Physicians can encourage lifestyle change before a diagnosis is made. We can all be more supportive of each other in these efforts. Congregations and communities can encourage and support healthy behaviors by educating and providing resources, opportunities, and places for healthy behavior.

What about Me?

Let's talk about health risks. If you have managed to make it to this point without contracting any significant illness, you may have already beat the odds. It's hard to believe that our health can change—we may not be as ready to defy death as a teenager seems to be, but it is tough to get bad news or to make changes to delay or prevent something that isn't real yet. After decades of neglect, if not abuse, we still expect our bodies to respond as they did when we were in our teens. Unfortunately, our bodies change as we age, even when we enjoy good physical health. Neglect and abuse don't just lead to early aging; they also result in disease that can seriously impair our quality of life.

After age 55, three out of four Americans are overweight. Being overweight is a risk factor for diabetes, heart disease, stroke, and some cancers (breast, prostate, colon, and uterine). Overweight aggravates arthritis and gout, results in high cholesterol and elevated blood pressure, causes problems with gallstones, and may result in sleep apnea. Extra weight aggravates bladder problems and increases the risk for kidney stones. It affects mental health, resulting in depression, eating disorders, distorted body image, and low self-esteem. Excess weight is not just a cosmetic problem; it has a significant impact on our quality of life.[5]

More than half of 55-year-olds have high blood pressure—typically a silent disease that frequently goes undiagnosed. Over time, high blood pressure damages the heart, kidneys, and eyes, and may result in stroke. At 55, one in four has high blood cholesterol, which leads to narrowing of the arteries—compromising blood flow to the heart, brain, and other organs. High blood pressure and cholesterol-clogged arteries are a major cause of impotence in men.

By age 55, one in eight Americans has diabetes. Diabetes is the major cause of blindness, amputations, and kidney failure. The bad news is that diabetes is on the rise as a result of this nation's obesity epidemic. Of greatest concern are our young adults and children, whose weight puts them at risk for diabetes at younger and younger ages. The longer one has diabetes, the greater the risk for the serious complications. Those in midlife have an opportunity to present a positive role model for the younger generation—children and grandchildren. Eating healthfully, exercising regularly, and being much more physically active is living life to the fullest. The good news is that changing your habits makes a difference. Losing weight and increasing one's activity can prevent or delay the onset of disease for years; in those with current disease, it can decrease symptoms, decrease the need for medications, and significantly improve the long-term outcome and quality of life. I am thankful that as I took on the responsibility and developed expertise in ministerial health and wellness, I realized I must take a good look at my own health. I have been blessed with good health for most of my life, but I had diabetes with my pregnancies and knew that I was at high risk for developing diabetes in later years. By improving my diet and increasing physical activity, as well as improving my emotional, intellectual, social, and spiritual health, I have lost weight and increased fitness and kept a lid on the diabetes.

Behavior Change

Most of us wait to get serious about making changes in our health until we get a serious warning. We wait until we are diagnosed with a disease such as high blood pressure, diabetes, or heart disease. Many wait until they have suffered a loss—had a heart attack, suffered a mild stroke, received a diagnosis of cancer, or had a close relative die.

What's the recipe for behavior change? Readiness is essential. This book is intended to prepare the ground for the seeds of change. Six stages of change are described by James Prochaska, psychologist and cancer researcher:

1. *Precontemplation.* Individuals in this stage have no intention to change, because they don't see any problem.

2. *Contemplation.* Here, individuals recognize a problem and begin to think about the need to change. They try to understand the causes of the problem and to consider solutions.
3. *Preparation.* This is the final stage before action, with plans to change within the next month. Making your commitment is an important step.
4. *Action.* At this point individuals are making visible changes—to stop smoking, start an exercise program, and change the foods they eat.
5. *Maintenance.* Change doesn't end with action. Unless one works actively on maintenance, relapse is likely.
6. *Termination.* At this point the changed behavior is no longer a problem for relapse.[6]

Anna Rose had worked at the retreat center for years. She started helping in the kitchen but was now in charge of meal preparation for the guests. She could walk to work and got along well with the director and the other staff. She felt good about working for a church-related retreat center, as her Catholic faith was strong. Anna Rose loved to cook, just as she loved to eat. She often received compliments for the meals she served. Besides the favorite recipes that her grandmother had prepared for the family, Anna Rose created some new favorites as well.

She gained weight steadily over the years—but so had her mother and sisters. She figured that weight gain was inevitable. Her mother and grandmother had both died of complications from diabetes, and that haunted her. She knew that excess weight was a contributing factor to the suffering of their last years. Recently, her younger sister had been diagnosed with diabetes, and that was a low blow. Anna Rose was not the only family member worried about diabetes, but she was very good at making up her mind. The kitchen staff knew that. She made up her mind that she had to lose weight. She was going to make every effort to keep diabetes at bay.

She began to read about diabetes and the recent information about the importance of exercise. She learned about the foods that cause a rapid rise of blood sugar and why that is important. She began to revise her recipes and meal plans. She decided to take the long way to work—a three-mile hilly walk. She told her sisters about her fear and her plan and asked them to support her and to keep her company on this journey. Two of them joined her. They picked a start date for their new lifestyle and even had a celebration of commitment the night before. Family members came and cheered them on.

Once they started, they discovered that the regimen was fun. The sisters became closer than they had ever been, enjoying the treats that nature provided on their trek to work and recreating menus to fit their healthy lifestyle. Anna Rose's apron strings, which once would barely stretch around her middle, were now tied in a neat bow. She had more energy than she had had in years. Her children said she glowed. After five months, Anna went to the clinic for a routine visit. She had refused to be weighed for years. The medical assistant started to ask to weigh her, then stopped in mid-sentence, remembering Anna Rose's avoidance. "No, I want to get weighed today," Anna said. "Hop right up then," said the medical assistant.

Anna Rose was 50 pounds lighter than the last recorded weight on the chart from five years ago. "Wow! Congratulations, Anna. How did you do it?"

"Well, I'm afraid of diabetes, so I just made up my mind. I asked my sisters to join me, I made a commitment to myself and my whole family, I made a plan to walk three miles a day and change my eating habits, I stuck to the plan, and I asked God for help." Anna's recipe for change has now resulted in a new Anna—100 pounds lighter and happy to share her story about how she changed her life.

Maybe Anna intuitively understood the importance of preparation because of many years of preparing meals. She followed the recipe for success: have a good reason to change, make a commitment and share it with others, get a buddy to join you, make a plan, stick to the plan, and ask God for help. American culture has devalued the concept of preparation or made it someone else's responsibility. We see a doctor when a problem becomes obvious or bad enough that it can no longer be denied, and we want a quick fix—antibiotics, diet pills, obesity surgery, liposuction, performance-enhancing drugs. We don't see the preparation anymore. Fast food is ready to eat. Clothes are ready-to-wear. Homes are ready to move in. We even pay for intensive classes of spoon-fed learning to help us pass college or graduate-school entrance exams. Successful change requires preparation. Let's review the challenges to health and wholeness and how to consider and prepare for change.

Weight/Nutrition

It is time to take weight and nutrition seriously as a culture and as a generation. Three out of four of those in midlife are already overweight. Most already have a medical problem related to being overweight. Many have family members who are also overweight. The first step to living well in retirement is to evaluate our eating habits.

Stephanie Paulsell, minister and teacher at Harvard Divinity School, writes in *Honoring the Body:*

> Is food our friend or our enemy? Is it a gift to be received with thankfulness or a problem to be mastered?

It is not surprising that our questions about food are nearly identical to our questions about our bodies. For what other daily activity is more integral to the practice of honoring the body than eating and drinking: How we understand our bodies—as friend or as enemy, as gift or as problem, as sacred or as repulsive, as temple of God's spirit or as a shell in which we are trapped—will influence how and what we eat and drink.[7]

Honoring the bodies that have served us well for decades makes good sense. Eating three meals and snacks each day is important. We need fuel to operate our brains and bodies, just as younger people do. The issue is that our caloric input must be equal to or less than our energy output. Most Americans will gain from one to two pounds every year. While that seems insignificant for a few years, by 20 years it can add up to 40 pounds! It is the creeping up of those pounds that "catches us by surprise" in midlife. We have to buy clothes in larger sizes. We have trouble getting up out of a chair or out of a car. We get heartburn from clothes that are too snug in the waist. We can't take the stairs without getting out of breath or sweating. So we take the elevator instead.

The way to avoid that one- or two-pound weight gain, as suggested by America on the Move (a national initiative for individuals and communities to improve health and quality of life) is to eat 100 fewer calories per day and to take 2,000 more steps a day.[8] The way to avoid the temptation to eat foods that are not nutritious or to overeat is to eat every four hours and to eat foods that will satisfy our hunger for a few hours. How much we eat depends on how active we are. What we should eat is best described in the "Healthy Food Pyramid" described by Walter Willett of the Harvard School of Public Health.[9]

Healthy Eating Pyramid

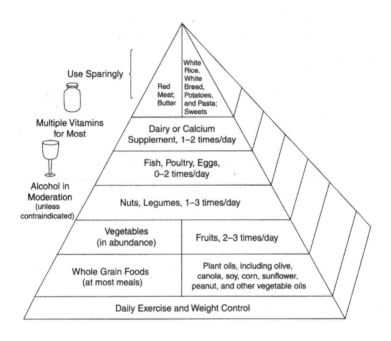

This pyramid is based on a foundation of daily weight control and exercise. Recommended carbohydrates are whole-grain foods such as oatmeal, whole-wheat bread, brown rice, fresh vegetables in abundance, and fruits. Fiber is carbohydrate that is not digested. It is present in edible plants such as fresh fruits and vegetables, grains, nuts, beans, and lentils. Plant oils are healthy fats and include olive, canola, soy, corn, sunflower, peanut, and other vegetable oils. Fatty fish such as salmon is another source of healthy fat. Fish, poultry, and eggs are important sources of protein. Nuts and legumes (black and navy beans, garbanzos) are a good source of protein, fiber, and vitamins. Low- or no-fat dairy products are a good source of calcium and protein. Be sparing in your diet with red meats, butter, and other animal fats, all of which are sources of saturated fat. Also avoid, or at least limit the quantity of, white rice, white potatoes, white bread, white pasta, and sweets. These are the foods that cause rapid rise and fall of blood sugar and have contributed to weight gain and diabetes. Replace them with brown rice, sweet potatoes, whole-grain bread, whole-grain pasta, and fresh fruits. These are foods that take longer to digest and result in a lower, slower rise of blood sugar. Sweet potatoes are low in calories, full of vitamins and minerals, and high in fiber. Fiber protects against heart disease, diabetes, diverticular disease of the colon, and constipation.

Having high cholesterol does increase your risk for heart disease. It is a waxy substance that can build up in blood vessels, causing them to narrow. There is "good" cholesterol (high-density lipoproteins or HDL) that is heart-protective and "bad" cholesterol (low-density lipoproteins or LDL) that clogs arteries. The amount of cholesterol in foods is not as important as the amount and types of fat. Eggs have suffered from a bad reputation because of the cholesterol in the yolks, but other ingredients in eggs are healthy. The bad actors among fats are the trans-fatty acids. These are present in commercially processed foods such as margarine, baked goods, or snack foods, and in commercially fried fast foods such as french fries or fried onion rings. Saturated fats are primarily animal fats that raise both the good and the bad cholesterol. The good fats are unsaturated fats—polyunsaturated (sunflower, corn, and soybean oils) and monounsaturated fats (canola, peanut, and olive oils). There is good evidence that high intake of either polyunsaturated or monounsaturated fat lowers the risk for heart disease. Other sources of good fats are fish (containing a polyunsaturated fat called omega-3) and nuts (containing monounsaturated fats). Remember that fats contain more calories than protein or carbohydrates.

Unless you are a vegetarian, it is easy to get enough protein in an American diet. The main problem with too much protein is the saturated fat that comes along with most meat. The advantage of protein is that it satisfies hunger for a longer period of time. Milk is a source of both protein and calcium. We all know that calcium helps to strengthen bones. So does weight-bearing exercise. Vitamin D is essential for bones to absorb calcium. Although we are not certain about the optimal amount of calcium, the current recommendation for adults over age 50 is 1200 milligrams of calcium a day. Other things you can do to protect your bones from osteoporosis (the weakening of bones from loss of calcium and aging) include decreasing caffeine intake, avoiding too much animal protein, and getting enough vitamin K (from green leafy vegetables). Although milk is a good source of calcium, too much milk can cause weight gain from fat and may be related to some types of cancer. (There are 300 milligrams of calcium in an eight-ounce glass of milk—whether skim or whole.)[10]

Physical Activity

Avoiding activity is the American way of life. We are surrounded by the tools of convenience. We microwave prepared foods, drive our cars to work, ride the elevator to our office, sit at a computer and talk on the phone, drive our cars home, pick up dinner from a fast-food restaurant on the way, sit at the table and turn on the television with the remote control, stack our dishes in the dishwasher, crash on the couch for more television, and climb into bed—only to repeat the same sequence almost every day.

Regular physical activity decreases the risk for heart disease, high blood pressure, stroke, diabetes, and many types of cancer. It also decreases anxiety and depression. Daily physical activity is the goal. That is best accomplished through a variety of planned exercise, along with increasing physical activity during your typical day. For example, walk when you are going less than a mile, or park further than usual from your destination. Take the stairs instead of the elevator, particularly when you are going up or down only one or two flights. Take walking breaks during the day instead of coffee breaks, or walk to the furthest bathroom.

Achieving health benefits from physical activity requires using a minimum of 1,000 calories of energy per week. How much time you will need to spend on physical activity depends on how intense the activity is. Moderate physical activity, recommended for 30 minutes most days of the week, includes walking briskly, pushing a lawn mower, dancing, swimming, bicycling on flat ground, yoga, weight training, golf (either wheeling or carrying a bag), gardening, housework, or carpentry. Vigorous activity (for 22 minutes) includes jogging, doing step aerobics, playing singles tennis, swimming laps, chopping wood, or shoveling heavy snow.

The good news is that it is never too late to become physically active. In response to a call to action in 1996 from Donna Shalala, then secretary of the U.S. Department of Health and Human Services, scientists from the Centers for Disease Control and Prevention wrote a guide to community action in promoting physical activity. "No matter how old you are, how unfit you feel, or how long you've been inactive, the scientific evidence shows that starting a more active lifestyle now through regular, moderate-intensity activity can make you healthier and improve your quality of life."[11]

In fact, regular physical activity or planned exercise has been shown to:

1. Minimize the physiologic changes associated with typical aging.
2. Contribute to psychological health and well-being.

3. Increase longevity and decrease the risk of several of the most common chronic diseases.

4. Be useful as primary or additional treatment for certain chronic diseases and to counteract specific side effects of standard medical care.

5. Assist in the prevention and treatment of disability.[12]

Remember the recipe for success from Anna: have a good reason to change, make a commitment, get a buddy to join you, make a plan, stick to the plan, and ask God for help. There are many good reasons to become physically active, but the more personal the reason, the better. One reason may be to avoid diabetes or high blood pressure, or to keep these in better control. Another reason may be to keep fit enough to play with grandchildren or to keep up with your spouse. The commitment also has to be real and the plan realistic. A commitment doesn't need to be videotaped—just tell someone, or put it in writing. Making a covenant as a statement of serious intent is a good approach. Many opportunities are available to join a group in physical activities, whether it is America on the Move, a local fitness club or walking club, or a regular activity with a buddy. The plan is how you intend to keep the covenant with a time line for how often and how long the regimen will be in effect.

Rest and Renewal

Sleep is too often considered the most expendable activity of our day. Other scheduled activities or work priorities demand attention, and when those activities are done or priorities met, or we can no longer keep our eyes open, we go to bed. Adults need from seven to nine hours of sleep every night. One sign that you are getting enough sleep is the ability to awaken naturally, not with an alarm clock. Sleep is controlled by light and darkness and by our daily activity. We are programmed to feel sleepy when it gets dark and when we have been awake for a certain period of time. Sleep provides rest; it is also a time when important hormones such as growth substances are secreted, blood pressure is lowered, some brain cells rest and some are activated, cells are repaired, and kidney functions change. Getting less sleep results in a "sleep deficit" over time, and the body's response is sleepiness. We risk becoming sleepy at times that demand attention—when we're driving a car or operating machinery. Inadequate nightly sleep cannot be "made up" on weekends or with naps. The constant vigilance to stay alert results in wear and tear on our bodies that put us at risk for other diseases. Inadequate sleep accelerates aging and the onset of diabetes. Sleep that is disrupted by discomfort, noise, bathroom needs, or irregular sleep patterns is not high-quality sleep. The stages of sleep follow a predictable pattern throughout an eight-hour period. There are five stages of sleep in a complete cycle lasting from about 90 to 110 minutes. The deepest stages of sleep (stages three and four) are most restorative—the blood pressure drops, breathing slows, hormones are released for growth and development, and energy is regained. The fifth stage of sleep (REM or rapid-eye movement) is the time when we dream. This stage provides energy to the body and brain and may contribute to storing memory. Tips to achieving restful sleep include:

- keeping a regular bedtime schedule,
- relaxing before bedtime,
- sleeping in a restful environment,
- avoiding caffeine, nicotine, and alcohol,
- avoiding heavy meals too close to bedtime, and

- exercising regularly at least three hours before bedtime.[13]

Our sleep needs don't change as we age, but maintaining restful, uninterrupted sleep becomes more difficult. Sleep is disturbed by illnesses such as heartburn, arthritis, and heart or lung disease. Hormone changes, as in menopause, and the need to urinate can interrupt sleep, as can other problems such as restless legs, snoring, or sleep apnea. People with sleep apnea stop breathing for several seconds, waking up many times during the night, often snorting or gasping for air. Depression and grief from bereavement or other losses deprive us of sleep. Daytime napping can result in nighttime awakening. Caffeine, nicotine, alcohol, and medications can adversely affect sleep. If you are having difficulty sleeping or are waking up tired, see your physician to review the possible causes and seek treatment.

We have rhythms of rest and activity that are a natural part of life. To take care of the body, we must recognize those rhythms and not fight them. By midlife, most of us know whether or not we are morning people. Some have their maximum time of energy in the morning. They look forward to getting up in the morning and to accomplishing tasks at the start of the day. These people do well with exercise first thing in the morning. Some of us drag ourselves reluctantly out of bed in the morning and are just hitting our stride by mid-afternoon or early evening. That is our time to exercise. Some people are nappers. Taking a 20-minute nap can increase energy and alertness, but don't use naps as a substitute for a good night's sleep.

What we cannot forget, however, is to take time to rest during the day and during our week. Minister and teacher Stephanie Paulsell writes:

God's own work is punctuated by contemplative moments of rest, in which God gazes upon what God has made and sees that it is good. God brings light into being; God pauses to see that it is good. God creates the flowering earth; God pauses to see that it is good. God's work is not uninterrupted labor, continuous exertion. God's way of working is unrushed, thoughtful, appreciative of what is emerging. Every exertion draws its strength from a profound desire for more life.[14]

If God made time in the day to contemplate and to appreciate the day, surely we can do the same. The beauty of God's earth should demand our attention and appreciation. Our work can surely benefit from thoughtful evaluation to see that it is good and purposeful. Such contemplation brings us physical and emotional health while bringing us closer to God.

Sex

We are created as sexual beings. The good news is that the third age can be a time to celebrate our sexuality. It is a time when we are more familiar with our bodies, more confident as individuals and in relationships, capable of a deeper love, and more understanding of the need for intimate connection. It is a time when we may have more time, or at least better control of our time. In an empty nest, time and space are back in the control of parents, most of the time.

According to Paulsell, "Birth, death and sex: these are the moments when we are perhaps best able to glimpse the connection between what is vulnerable and what is sacred. For sex that is exquisitely consoling and reflects God's desire for our freedom and our good can only be had when two people make themselves vulnerable to one another."[15] Sexual activity is relaxing, relieves stress, and creates intimacy. It is a time to express that ultimate connection and deepest caring with the one you love. Sexual health is associated with happiness and well-being. Studies have shown that frequency and enjoyment of sexual intercourse are significant predictors of longevity.

Middle age is also a time when aging or chronic disease can begin to affect sexual response. One study has found that more than half of a population of men between 40 and 70 years of age had some degree of erectile dysfunction.[16] Any illness can have an impact on sexual interest and function, especially high blood pressure, diabetes, and depression. Additionally, medications used to treat many illnesses, as well as cigarettes, alcohol, and street drugs, can have a negative effect on sexual function. Certainly the hormone changes related to age and menopause, including similar changes in men, can affect sexual arousal and response. If this is a concern for you, it is important to have a full discussion with a medical professional who can give helpful advice or prescribe effective treatments.

The important thing to know is that sexuality is an important aspect of health and quality of life. At any age, adults remain sexual beings with desires, fantasies, and active sex lives. An American Association for Retired Persons (AARP) survey of sexuality in older adults found that 67 percent of men and 57 percent of women indicated that satisfying sex is an important part of their lives.[17] Six out of 10 men and women between 45 and 69 years of age report having sex once a week. In the 60-to-74-year-old group, 30 percent of men and 24 percent of women reported having sex once a week. Of those 75 years and older, one out of four have sex weekly. Nine out of 10 men and women indicated that a good relationship with their partner was important to their quality of life, and most older couples found their mates more attractive as they aged.

Jean had gained 35 pounds in 20 years of marriage—10 for each pregnancy and five for good measure. She and her husband, Phil, had been avid bikers early in their marriage, but he was spending more and more time at work. Her daughter Jennifer was a runner, and Jean decided to join Jennifer's runs, but on her bike. It was hard work at first, but soon she was enjoying the time with her daughter in the fresh air. It became a habit that continued after Jennifer left for college. Slowly but steadily she lost 20 pounds and discovered how much easier it was to do normal daily activities. She had begrudgingly accepted achy knees and stiffness as a sign of aging but discovered what a difference 20 fewer pounds made.

Later during seminary, Jean took a water aerobics class in the neighborhood with Ellen. They were both struggling with long days of sitting in class and evenings of reading and writing. At lunch one day they decided that what they needed was some physical activity to keep their brain cells awake. It turned out to be an enjoyable way to connect and to share experiences and ideas. Jean learned that she had much more energy when she had a regular year-round exercise plan.

There is no fountain of youth—no magic potion to erase years. Genes, life experiences, and aging are factors affecting our health over which we have little control. The majority of elements that have an impact on our health, however, are our lifestyle behaviors—what we eat, how physically active we are, how much regular sleep we get, and whether we use unhealthy substances. These are factors we can control. You can maximize youthfulness by doing an assessment of your current lifestyle and state of health and making positive changes. You might even enjoy it!

For Reflection

1. What is the state of your middle-aged body? One way to find out is to take an online test at *www.realage.com.*

2. What is most likely to be the cause of your death?
3. How has your lifestyle changed in the past 20 years? How are you planning to change your current habits (physical activity, nutrition, rest)?
4. How is your sex life? If you have a partner, what does your partner think/feel about it?

3

Where's the Joy?
Emotional Health

Terry Hershey, Protestant minister and gardener, writes of the risk of giving yourself completely to your work and losing sight of your emotional essence: "We go about our merry and hectic way, accumulating and weighing, measuring and posturing, hoping that the balance sheet of life judges us with kindness. Until that one day when you look into the mirror and ask yourself 'Why?' and you decide then and there to set about reclaiming that which has been lost—namely, you."[1]

Unfortunately, many of us don't stop to ask the question until we are nearing retirement. For some, that may be too late. We all know the stories of those whose lives were focused on their job and who were dead six months after retirement. Emotions have a significant impact on our health and wholeness.

Jean was a happy child and teenager. Church was a second home for her, as her mother was very active in the church and often brought the children along. Jean loved learning about the Bible and singing in the choir. She began her teaching career by assisting and then teaching vacation Bible school as a teenager. Her pastor was supportive and encouraging. He was the one who suggested that she would make an excellent teacher and told her that she had many gifts to offer the church. Although she was pleased by his words, she was a little disappointed because what she really wanted in her heart was to be like him.

Years later, Jean was at a retirement party for Barb, a favorite teacher in her school. Barb had put in her 30 years and was retiring from public education and going back to school to concentrate on creative writing. Barb had been a mentor for Jean. Barb's love for the children and her enthusiasm for teaching were contagious. Many had been surprised by her announcement last year that this would be her final year of teaching. No one had ever heard a word of complaint, and everyone had benefited from Barb's passion for her work. She had started evening classes in writing and had recently had a story published in a local magazine. Jean hugged Barb and said, "I'm really going to miss you. We have had so much fun together." Barb held her by the shoulders and said, "Jean, I have loved teaching, and the children have meant everything to me. But my dream has been to be a writer, and it's time for me to follow my heart."

Although Jean cared for the children she taught, one day was indistinguishable from another, and she was having difficulty getting out of bed in the morning to get to school. Her own children were in high school, needing her less for the routines of life but more as a sounding board for their emotional struggles with finding their own identities. Some days she felt as though she were trying to walk through knee-deep snow. She shared these feelings with her husband, but he was struggling with his own job and unable to listen without jumping in to make comparisons to his own difficulties. That summer she knew she needed to do some soul-searching and to make changes to survive another year of teaching.

Jean had taken a few days to go home to see her mother, who was slowing down because of arthritis. While there, she found herself near her home church. She slipped in the back of the church and sat down in a pew. The organist was practicing, and Jean began to hum. As she sat there, she felt a lightening of the heaviness in her chest and a sense of warmth throughout her body. She felt at home as she had not for years. Sinking into this warmth, she began to feel a flutter of emotions rising to the surface. She closed her eyes, asking God, "What does this mean? What am I to do?" The answer did not come easily. Jean had opened the door to her heart and to feelings that she had suppressed for years. Her life had become one of emotional numbness, and this awakening was as painful as the "pins and needles" experienced as a foot recovers from being sat on. She would awaken each morning wondering if the pain would be unbearable or if she would be able to function.

Time reduced the pain, and counseling helped her gradually return to full functioning. The process resulted in a painful divorce but also to a certainty that she needed to go to seminary. Her heart was Christ's, and her home was in the church. She knew it now, and for the first time in years she had a clarity of vision—who she was and whose she was.

Cultivate Positive Emotions

Emotions are a gift from God. How we display them depends on our culture and our personality. Cultural differences may be rooted in age, gender, ethnicity, country of origin, socio-economic class, or education. Some people express emotions with passion, and others are stoic. The people we are with and where we are make a difference in how we express ourselves. We are more natural around our family than with strangers. We act differently in same-gender or same-age groups than in mixed groups. We act differently in situations of distress—some wailing and flailing and others silent and immobile. Our brain—the birthplace of our emotions—and its connections to our body are so miraculous and complex that we cannot fully understand them. We are capable of hysterical laughter that produces tears, choking, belly pain, and eventual prostration, just as we are capable of profound grief and sadness that can totally immobilize us mentally and physically.

Happiness is what we all strive for in life—not just the giddiness we may experience at a birthday party or watching a funny movie—but the joy that comes from living a full life, one that is satisfying and productive. This contentment is an outcome of living with the Wholeness Wheel in balance (see page 5). We feel happy when we are feeling physically well and able, emotionally satisfied, intellectually challenged, socially enriched, vocationally purposeful, and spiritually blessed. Happiness comes when you are yourself, in work, worship, and play.

Think about your happiest moment. Maybe it was a childhood Christmas memory. Maybe it was the day you asked your loved one to marry you, or the birth of your first child. Perhaps it was the day of your ordination or the celebration of 25 years of ministry or 25 years of happy marriage. Have you had days when you just could not keep a smile off your face? When you felt as though you were floating along without touching the ground? When if you opened your mouth, laughter slipped out—not because something was funny but because you couldn't suppress the happy noise? On those days, we praise the Lord for life experienced to the fullest. While we cannot enjoy the same intensity of feeling every day, we can strive to live our life in a way that brings us daily happiness.

Some people find joy in the details of daily life that many of us find mundane or frustrating. Positive emotional health comes from the ability to celebrate the beauty in the details. If you are a morning person, a characteristic sometimes acquired with age, you may delight in the music that awakens you, the golden light that fills the room as the sun comes up, the dewy clean colors of nature in the early sunlight, the fresh and happy faces of those who greet you. You can certainly find joy at the end of the day in the tail-wagging greeting of your pets or the hugs of loved ones. Savor a glass of wine or a delicious meal while watching the intense colors as they deepen with the setting sun. Rejoice in a late-afternoon or evening walk or run as you observe the changing seasons or greet your neighbors.

While happiness is important, other aspects of positive emotional health also matter. Some say that intelligence is the main contributor to success in life or work, whereas others raise the concept of "emotional intelligence" as the primary factor. Emotional intelligence includes the skills of self-awareness, self-management, social awareness, and relationship management.[2] Positive emotional health includes these dimensions—individual and social wellness, including awareness of self and others, and the ability to manage personal and interpersonal emotions.

Awareness of emotions, which lies at the heart of emotional intelligence, is an essential ingredient for positive emotional health. Taking time to appreciate the beauty around us and to feel the positive emotions that result are healthy approaches to cultivating such awareness. Many of us were taught as children to name our feelings, but as we age, our experiences and feelings become more complex and naming them becomes more difficult. At times, we may be so overcome by many emotions that it is hard to sort them out—never mind manage them. Pastors, living with the demands of ministry and the emotions of parishioners, may shut down their own feelings as a coping mechanism from the emotional and physical demands of their position. Some, like Jean, are so bombarded with the chores of everyday life that they have to suppress emotions to stay on task. While that may work temporarily, it is not the way to emotional health. We need to take the time to recognize and acknowledge our emotions—anger, sadness, frustration, fear, boredom, shame, joy, relief, misery, satisfaction. It is when we don't recognize and deal with our emotions that we are unable to make changes toward positive emotional health. Without those changes, we store up negative emotions that eat away at other dimensions of our health, and we continue on a path that will only become more difficult.

People with positive emotional health are aware of their thoughts, feelings, and behaviors and are able to manage them. They feel good about themselves and have healthy relationships. They keep problems in perspective by recognizing their emotional response to a perceived problem and by dealing with the cause, whether that means developing new skills, making changes in themselves, or working things out with others. Developing this emotional intelligence takes experience. Most of us in middle age have experienced a wide range of emotions and the life events related to those emotions. We have learned by trial and error how to manage them and have discovered what effect our emotions have on others. One hopes we have developed the ability to take a moment before reacting to consider the consequences of our actions. We have learned that being out of balance—tired, hungry, emotionally fragile—means that we have less control. We know that alcohol and drugs cloud or exaggerate emotions and rob us of control. We have cultivated a network of supportive relationships. We recognize that obsessing over problems is not the answer and that naming the problem and dealing with it is the way toward positive emotional health.

The third age of life should be a time to kick back and enjoy life. This enjoyment doesn't come automatically with retirement or the attainment of a certain age, even though we may feel that we have earned it. We will continue to be active—whether that means full-time or part-time work, parenting, caring for parents, learning new skills, or taking up old hobbies. We will continue to experience the full range of emotions—loss brings sadness, change brings frustration, disease may bring fear, grandchildren bring joy. Maturity brings a level of confidence and calm from life experience. Happiness is sweeter, love is deeper, laughter more precious, tears more frequent but not bitter. It is a time to celebrate what has been, what is, and what will be. Memories of growing up, growing in faith, and growing in love are recalled and treasured. We have a deeper understanding of the importance of family and of vocation. We spend less energy on trying to get ahead in life through career advancement, acquiring material goods, or raising a family. The last third is time to explore the meaning of life. It is time to savor precious moments. By the last third of life, most of us have acquired the ability to reflect on the importance of relationships and the purpose of work. We feel closer to God because of the richness of life experiences and the ability to listen and speak to God.

Expressing Our Emotions

Emotions are to be experienced. We have emotions because of the complex and miraculous wiring of our brains. Becoming aware of emotions is essential. But it is expressing them appropriately, or managing them, that keeps our emotional boat afloat on the shifting waves of experience. Exhibiting the facial expressions, body language, and sounds that match our emotions serves to clue others in to how we are feeling. That allows us to communicate meaningfully with others. Newborn babies learn quickly to recognize faces. They also learn to mimic expressions and sounds. We can often recognize emotions in our loved ones by their posture or their tone of voice. We make decisions every day based on our assessment of another's emotions. We approach or not, strike up a conversation or not, bring up a touchy topic or not, cross to the other side of the street or reach out to help.

> For Jean, the demands of daily life with her own children and the children of others consumed her energy. Coping with the many moods and demands of her students left her with

barely enough energy to feed and care for her own children and her husband, with little remaining for fun. To get through day after day, she boxed up her emotions and put them on a shelf to be opened sometime in the future. That worked for a while, but when the needs of her mother took her out of her own context and brought her to the church in a state of vulnerability, the box popped open and emotions started to sneak out. Some were positive and some painful, but once the box was opened, she couldn't get the lid closed again.

"Stuffing" emotions leads to illness and even to death. Regardless of our cultural background or individual personality, it is essential for our health to learn to express emotions in appropriate ways. Repressed anger may lead to substance abuse or to physical or emotional abuse of others. Anger can trigger a heart attack. Depression doubles the risk of a second heart attack. Hopelessness has been found to predict heart attacks and death.[3] How we handle our emotions affects not only our physical health but our relational health as well. When we don't express our emotions or share our feelings with others, our words and actions can be misunderstood or misinterpreted. At the same time, if we live in an angry or sad state most of the time, focusing on the negatives and forgetting the positives, we are out of balance, and others stop responding to our needs. Although we want to learn to express *all* our emotions, we need to find a way to express and experience joy, peace, and hope to foster our relationships and enjoy life.

If we aren't in the practice of expressing emotions, we may not recognize negative feelings and may have difficulty dealing effectively with the issues causing them. If we avoid feeling and expressing our positive emotions, we are missing out on the fullness of life. We are unlikely to experience the depth of love without risking loss or feeling anger. There will be days when we are laughing hysterically with others at the fun in life and other days when we shed tears at life's tragedies or personal losses. Having experienced frustration with miscommunication or misunderstanding makes those moments of true understanding or emotional connection even sweeter. Pastors may be discouraged from showing emotions, as it may be seen as unprofessional, or as a demonstration of weakness or vulnerability. If emotional numbness has been a way of life during one's public ministry, it may be difficult to reawaken the awareness and revive the expression of emotions in retirement.

One way of coping with strong emotions is to stifle them and eventually not to feel them. Individuals who have undergone traumatic experiences, such as serving in combat in Vietnam or Iraq, or being violently attacked, may suffer from post-traumatic stress disorder (PTSD). To survive, they need to suppress the overwhelming emotions experienced during the trauma, but they continue to relive those emotions in "flashback" memories or dreams for months and years afterward. Unfortunately, behavior that develops as a helpful initial coping mechanism can become problematic. Individuals with PTSD often develop a psychological numbness—a dulling of the experience of all strong feelings. These individuals are viewed by others as uncaring or inappropriately unemotional; they lose their ability to experience fully even the important, positive emotions of living. Individuals suffering from the symptoms of PTSD require professional treatment and counseling to help address fear, to develop more healthy coping mechanisms, and to reintroduce positive emotions.

Age brings more life experiences but also greater wisdom in understanding and appreciating those experiences. The nice thing about having lived several decades is that one cares less what others think. It is easier to live more in the present and to experience each day more fully. One can laugh with greater gusto and cry freely without hiding tears. It's natural to get down on the floor and play with children as one of them. In reaching out to others to make connections, one does not hesitate to let others know how one feels. That is the privilege of the third age. As long as the expression of those emotions is respectful of others, one has earned the right to loosen up. In addition to being freer with emotions, one can be more focused on cultivating positive emotions. While the emotions of youth include frustration, anger, anxiety, uncertainty, and other feelings that result from discovery of self in relation to others, maturity brings more comfort with who we are and more personal peace, joy, and hope.

Seeking Peace

In his book *Seeking Peace,* Johann Christoph Arnold, minister and spiritual guide, writes, "Peace is a life-giving power. It heals what is broken, replenishes what is used up, and unleashes what is knotted and bound up. Peace brings hope where there is despair, harmony where there is discord, love where there is hatred."[4] It is easy to be angry—when things don't go smoothly, when things break, when other people's driving annoys, when the daily news disappoints and exasperates, when terrorist threats loom. There are opportunities for anger every day. The availability of 24-hour news radio or television can be a constant reminder of the world's woes. We may experience despair because life has treated us unfairly— we think of a lost loved one, lost opportunities, physical or emotional abuse by others. We have to learn deliberately to look for the hopeful and to tune out the discouraging.

A first step in seeking peace is to be aware of one's own anger or despair and of the widespread discord and hatred in the world. While it is healthy to express emotions, it is important to learn to vent negative emotions appropriately—especially anger. Anger can lead to violence, broken relationships, divorce, or the loss of a job. Anger turned inward can lead to physical symptoms, including headaches, heart attacks, or ulcers. We can't avoid anger completely. To develop ways of controlling or deflecting anger away from others, however, we want to be aware of the states that make us vulnerable to anger. Hunger and fatigue, and especially sleep deprivation, make many people irritable and set off their short fuse. Recognize the warning signs of your anger. Many of us feel the rush of adrenalin that precedes an angry outburst. Learn how to redirect that rush toward other outlets like punching the air, taking a walk, or shaking out the tension.

Many of us feel despair at times about the hatred in our world. Sometimes we should be angry at the violence and direct that anger into positive action. Strong emotions produce an energy that can be applied positively to make a difference. We have seen individuals turn the devastating emotions of the loss of a child into a passion to work toward change, so that others don't have to endure their experiences. We can't help but be sad about personal or other losses. Releasing tears is therapeutic, but wallowing in tears is self-defeating and does not honor the memory of those missed. Sometimes professional help is needed to deal with our emotions, to regain the energy needed to address the issues or relationships troubling us, and to move forward.

> When Jean's emotional box popped open, she asked for help. If circumstances had been different, she might have sought help from other resources, but seated in God's house, she reached out for God. As she did, she knew she was home. Although the pain of reawakening emotions was difficult, she felt a sense of hope. But she recognized that she needed help to face these emotions, to make sense of her life, and to make the necessary changes to find joy again.

Regularly practicing tranquility of the mind and relaxation of the body paves the way for maintaining a sense of peacefulness, even in times of stress. Many whose lives are defined by their occupation find that nothingness is fatal—when there is no job to go to and no sense of tranquility. There is a difference between enjoying tranquility and having nothing to do. Relaxation and peace of mind bring energy and direction that will encourage you to create purposeful experiences in retirement. Relaxation exercises are in fact intense times of focus—a focus on physically releasing tension and clearing the mind. Done regularly, these exercises make it natural and easy to release accumulated tension and to promote physical and emotional health. Meditation or prayer—feeling God's love, asking for forgiveness, seeking God's peace, releasing burdens, praying for others, accepting God's grace and forgiveness—practiced regularly, these also bring health. We hunger for peace, and yet we know that God's peace, which is beyond our understanding, protects our minds and our hearts in Christ Jesus.

Paul gives us even more specific instructions in Philippians 4:8 to think about those things that are true, honorable, just, pure, pleasing, commendable, excellent, or worthy of praise. These things are realities of our everyday world that do not make the news, but thinking about them brings us closer to God and to God's peace. We have the opportunity to hear God's voice in the silence and to understand what the goals and mission of this time of life are. If we listen and understand, we can begin to meet them. Our relationship with God and our understanding of the purpose of work in retirement bring a sense of peace.

This work might be serving others and developing new relationships by volunteering in public schools, museums, hospitals, or churches. It might involve going back to school to learn new skills or to acquire knowledge. It may require healing old wounds or relationships by working with a therapist. We can spend "quality time" with grandchildren, nieces, or nephews. Using talents that have been hidden away during working years—musical, artistic, mathematical, or practical—can be rejuvenating and can lead to other venues of work.

Write a journal or a book to tell stories for your family, or write about your work to inspire or inform others.

Retiring from a lifelong occupation is a dramatic change and can produce anxiety when one has devised no plan for life after retirement. In our culture you are defined by your work. But being retired doesn't define you. Being retired means you are not constrained to define yourself in terms of your occupation. When you are asked what you do, your response should reflect what is unique about you and what you are passionate about:

"I'm a grandmother, and I love helping my children by getting to know my grandchildren as very special individuals."

"I'm a teacher, and I teach English as a second language to new Americans."

"I'm an artist, and I take photographs of native wildflowers."

"I'm a woodworker, and I love to create beautiful and useful objects from wood."

"I'm a gardener, and I'm creating a perennial garden that will have beautiful flowers and plants all year round."

Knowing who you are in retirement, perhaps with even more integrity than your occupational role, brings a sense of peace.

Feeling Joy

The psalmist prayed, "Restore to me the joy of your salvation, and sustain in me a willing spirit" (Ps. 51:12). We do not feel the fullness of joy without suffering. There can be no Easter without a crucifixion. Can you imagine the joy and the wonder of those who loved Jesus, seeing him alive again? Through Christ's crucifixion, we have the promise of eternal life—what better reason to be joyful? Joy is not mere happiness, but the deepest expression of gratitude for life and richness of emotion. It is a feeling acknowledging at once the beauty of what is known and the wonder of what is unknowable.

Unfortunately, from 8 to 20 percent of older adults in the community experience depressive symptoms.[5] Depression is more than just sadness. We all experience sadness and can even be overwhelmed by despair at times. Depression is the inability to see the beauty in life and the loss of wonder at the unknown. Severe depression is our state when joy has left us and we are so overwhelmed by sadness, despair, or helplessness that we cannot get out of bed, leave the house, or do anything more than just survive. When we are depressed, we can't remember enjoying anything, we have no interest in friends or family, and nothing is funny or even interesting. We are obsessed by feelings of sadness, hopelessness, and helplessness. Priest and devotional writer Henri Nouwen describes depression this way: "There is a deep hole in your being like an abyss. You will never succeed in filling that hole, because your needs are inexhaustible. You have to work around it so that gradually the abyss closes."[6]

The good news is that depression can be helped by medication and by counseling. The problem is that people who are depressed are so weighed down by emotion and fatigue that they don't recognize the problem or don't have the energy to do anything to address it. It usually takes the intervention of someone who cares to ask, "How are you feeling?" or who can gently tell you, "I think you need help," and then make an appointment and take you there. Most people who have depression welcome help but need support and encouragement to seek out treatment or to continue in counseling.

Successful treatment of depression lifts the cloud over our eyes, allowing us once again to see the beauty in life. It releases the unbearable pressure so that we can breathe again and begin to move toward health. It brings us to the edge of the abyss so that we can look out and see hope. It takes time to reclaim the joy of living, but we can see its promise through the love in our family's eyes, the smell of a newborn baby, the colors of the rainbow, the warmth of a familiar hymn. Eventually we are able to reach out to make a difference in others' lives because we have found joy in ours. Living to middle age has given us the opportunity to experience joys and sorrows. It has taught us how to accept emotions for what they are, has given us greater awareness and appreciation, and has taught us better management. We recognize the situations that give rise to negative emotions, and we know that we have a choice in how we react. We also know that moments of pure happiness may be brief but are invaluable. Lasting joy comes from truly knowing who we are and fulfilling our God-given promise. It comes from sharing this promise with others around us and rejoicing in their gifts that complement ours. It comes from the knowledge of the infinite potential each of us has in concert with others to make a difference in our community and our world. It comes with the celebrations of these gifts and the successes we may have in making the world a more joyful place.

Live in Hope

> The work that Jean did to air out and try on those packed-away emotions paved the way for her vocational and other life changes. She learned to recognize and to experience her emotions, to seek balance in her life, and to appreciate the value of physical activity in achieving that balance. She reclaimed her personal energy and used it more strategically. She set new goals for the future and had hope. Living and working through the pain and anxiety brought her to a new sense of joy and peace.

Paul writes in Romans 15:13, "May the God of hope fill you with all joy and peace in believing, so that you may abound in hope by the power of the Holy Spirit." We can live joyful lives and seek and find peace personally and in our relationships, but hope demands belief in the future. As Christians, our hope is in Christ—that through his death and resurrection we will have eternal life. The power of the Holy Spirit fills us with hope and energy to share the love of God and the power of the cross. In the third age we are closer to realizing the reality of death and of eternal life. Living closer to that hope should make us want to share that hope with others. Living as an example of that hope is an inspiration for those around us—family, friends, and community. It is in this community of believers that we find hope for the world. Many roles await us in that community—depending on the gifts we bring.

We have hope for eternal life, but also for life on this earth. Through baptism each of us is a new creation in Christ. As God's creation we have unlimited potential. What more dramatic picture of hope do we see than the sight of a baby being born or baptized? Our potential does not diminish with age. In fact, our potential is possibly more realizable. Much energy and time are required to develop as infants, toddlers, children, teenagers, and young adults. As middle-aged adults, we have mastered many of the routine tasks of life. But we still find opportunities for growth, and our energy for change or growth can be focused. This is no time to vegetate. This God-given potential is a gift—not one to be used up and discarded but a gift that is ours until we die. Having hope means that we continue to believe in a better world, and as long as we are alive, we continue to strive toward that hope. For some, hopefulness means continuing to work in some capacity. For others it means to continue to learn, to create, or to love and to share. God is the source of all hope, and we are God's children—regardless of age. We hope for eternal life, peace on earth, happiness for our children, and a healthier community. Having hope and acting on it provide the spark to light the fire that makes this world a better place.

When we think about health, we think first about physical health and its importance to living a meaningful life. In reality, emotional health is probably of greater importance. The real goal, however, is to remember the Wholeness Wheel and to seek a healthy balance.

For Reflection

1. Write or tell the story of your happiest moment. Think about how you can recapture that feeling on a regular basis.
2. Describe what brings you joy in your life. How do you express that joy?
3. What challenges do you have in managing your emotions?
4. How will you introduce yourself in retirement? What makes you "you," and how will you express that identity in that time of your life?
5. What do you hope for, and how are you actively living your life toward that hope?

4

Use It or Lose It
Intellectual Health

"Lifelong learner" is a term that has come to define today's generation of middle-agers. We are an educated population, and we have experienced change at such a rapid pace that to stay current and functional, we have to continue to learn. Our brains are wonderfully complex computers with an apparently infinite capacity for continual change and learning. As a generation, we have read books, attended schools, worshiped in churches, lived through wars, seen our families grow, experienced jobs and careers. We have seen books morph into electronic books, schools adopt "distance learning," and churches televise worship services and project hymn texts, PowerPoint slides, still photos, and videos on large screens in the worship space. Military strategists have set aside hand-to-hand combat in favor of computer-guided missile strikes. Family members have left their birthplaces for schools and jobs around the world. Workers have come to expect multiple job and career changes. Our brains enable us to learn new skills in new and unfamiliar situations and to adapt to change while continuing to hold onto what we value. In this world of increasingly rapid change, intellectual health is essential to our wholeness.

Michael is a true intellectual—not the pompous nose-in-the-air intellectual that we all know, but someone who gets giddy about new information or new insights into old information.

Knowledge is his holy grail. Michael took Latin in high school and loved it. He took Greek as his required language in college and started on the road to seminary. He had discovered that it was not just the mastery of the language that excited him, but the sense of mastery that knowing the language gave him in his understanding of Scripture. Hebrew was next, and a major in classical language resulted.

Those of us who knew Michael in seminary expected him to be a professor of Old Testament at the seminary—until our last year. His internship was a time of transformation. He fell in love. Not with Jan—that happened before internship—but with congregational life. He loved preaching every Sunday, planning worship, celebrating the sacraments, making hospital calls. He even loved council meetings. As he carried out his parish duties, he saw that the language of faith he had studied for years was alive and meaningful today. Because he was passionate about his ministry, he continued to study, not just for his own knowledge, but to answer the probing questions that came from the congregations and from his own family.

Mentors have also been a powerful influence in Michael's life. He kept in touch with his professors from seminary over the years, returning for continuing education, collaborating on articles for several publications, and eventually joining the faculty as adjunct professor in systematic theology. His internship supervisor became a lifelong friend and advisor for congregational and personal issues. They often planned to attend conferences together so that they could also spend personal time catching up. They shared a love of art history and visited museums together. One year they and their wives went on a memorable European seminar on sacred art through Germany, Italy, and France.

Michael had a dream of telling the gospel story through art. He developed a popular series of presentations using artwork to tell the story in new and different ways. He drew not only on the familiar paintings of Mary or of the crucifixion, but also on art of many different times and styles. The presentations particularly captured the attention of the youth, and the demand for his talks grew. Just last year, Michael took a six-month sabbatical. He used the time to plan and start a series of books depicting the gospel through art for different ages, using different styles of art. He is planning to finish the first book this year and is looking forward to retiring from his full-time call to have more time to spend on his books.

Learning Languages

Computers have transformed life as we know it. Some of us have lived without them and also remember when they were large enough to take up a whole building. Many of us now carry them in our pockets or purses. Not only do we use them to organize our lives and to store and help us track down needed information, our pocket computers and cell phones also connect us to almost anyone anywhere. We have had to learn to use this technology. Now we have to learn how to control it and how to use it to enhance our lives rather than letting it control us. The ability to use a computer, however, does not mean that we are able to use computer technology to communicate.

Communication begins with crying and then advances to simple words—"Up!" "Milk!" "Cookie!"—to get our needs met. The next important words are signs of exerting our personality: "No!" and then "Why?" Then we begin to tell stories—some truthful and some not. We use language as a means to separate ourselves from our parents' generation or to claim our identity. As we continue in school and in life, we need to develop a mastery of the spoken and written language to communicate our thoughts, knowledge, and plans. As middle-aged adults, we can communicate about the practical—our daily aches and pains or the price of milk—and we can communicate about the meaningful: feelings and life experiences. We can communicate efficiently to get the job done, or imaginatively to entertain or engage others. We can repetitively chant liturgy that comes from deeply embedded memory, or we can pray spontaneously from the heart.

Many of us find that as we grow older, we become more reflective and have more time to think deeply about the meaning of our existence. We have also developed significant relationships and want to communicate with those who have become important to us about what we have been learning. As we learn to think differently about ourselves and our world, we also begin to use language differently. Rather than relying primarily on the efficient, terse prose that is intended to get work done, many of us find great delight in personal journal keeping or letter writing that conveys emotions, tells our life story, or explores our purpose in the world. A few find that writing poetry is an essential means of distilling emotions and experiences into a spare rhythm that speaks to them intellectually and viscerally. Some use the wisdom gained from years of experience to write helpful articles, books, textbooks, meditations, songs, or prayers as guides to others in their lives or vocations.

> Michael's love of language led him to a better understanding of the Scriptures. His love of God's word led him to learn more about how to tell the story—through sermons, Bible studies, conversations, travel, and art. It was a journey that eventually led him to explore works of art and finally to help translate the visual message into words that would enlighten and educate many more.

Learning another language is one way of refining, expanding, and re-examining our native tongue. It is certainly good exercise for the brain. Unlike children, who seem to have an infinite capacity to mimic and become facile with words of any language, adults who set out to learn a new language have to struggle against their entrenched language of origin. They have to endure pure rote memorization, word by word, until the words become phrases and the phrases become natural. When my daughter left for college with her two best friends, all three fluent in Spanish, their three mothers decided to take a plunge and learn Spanish as a way to ease the transition in our families and to have fun. None of us had studied it before. We entertained the notion of communicating with our daughters in Spanish. Well, we learned the alphabet and the basics. Parroting back the teacher's words was easy; answering questions was another matter. The exercise was a reality check about the sluggishness of the aging brain, but a wonderful social and intellectual adventure.

Language is useful in many ways, but a time comes when we want to use language to leave a legacy. Now is the time to tell our stories, to share our feelings, to impart the wisdom gained from experience in ways that will be heard and remembered. Most often we pass on that legacy, without even realizing it, to those who are closest to us. The legacy might not be so much in what we say as in how we communicate. Watch grandparents with their young grandchildren. They are not as likely to talk to them in baby talk as they are to speak to them from the heart in a calm and soothing voice about life or feelings or the day. A special kind of communication links grandparents and grandchildren. It is direct but rarely scolding or meaningless. A combination of words, facial expression, and posture conveys a warmth that envelops a rock-solid trustworthiness. Grandparents or other elder family members or friends are less likely to be swayed by daily frustrations or the emotions of the moment than a child's parents are; they are more patient and dependable. This may be an idealized picture, but it reflects a maturity that comes with having lived a full life and having observed or participated in the raising of another generation.

This third age is a time to use that maturity for the benefit of generations to come. Use the language and communication skills gained over decades to make a difference in the world. Volunteer in a public school or teach Sunday school—patience and attention are qualities in great demand for our children. If working with children is not your strong suit, teach English as a second language to new Americans who need the practical language for daily survival, or teach adults the creative language of prayer, poetry, or prose. Be the voice of reason at community or congregational committee meetings. Enrich others with your experience and wisdom, but don't forget your continual need for personal enrichment. Read things that you have not had time to read. Expand your knowledge about other people, other places, other religions, science or technology, animals, space exploration, art, history. The possibilities for learning are endless. Tell others what you have learned or join a discussion group to share information and converse about life. Go back to classes to learn new skills and to exchange thoughts and knowledge with others of different generations. We continue to grow in our understanding of ourselves and others through language—written, heard, and thought.

Using Our Senses to Learn

We don't learn in a vacuum. Learning is accomplished by reading, listening, watching, and touching. Life is experienced through our senses—sight, smell, sound, taste, and touch. We interpret those sensory experiences through our miraculous brain. New sensations stimulate us and help us to learn. Familiar sensations satisfy and comfort us. We have difficulty with our sanity if we are deprived of sensations. The media have reminded us of the use of sensory deprivation as a tool of torture. But what about the constant noise of our current daily life? We must contend with the drone of traffic noise, the meaningless background chatter of television, the incessant ringing of the cell phone, or the isolation of hearing music through individual headphones. We don't use our senses to their fullest capacity. We are too busy looking at our computer or television screen to notice the changing sky or the sparkling stars. We dull our taste buds with too much salt and a lack of variety. We do not hear the evening sounds through the closed windows and the noise of air conditioning. We miss the subtle early changes of spring as we rush through traffic to reach our destination. The third age is a time of life to reawaken the senses. Buy season tickets to the orchestra or opera, take nature walks, learn to throw pottery, take cooking lessons. Sign up for a photography class and begin to photograph your favorite things—grandchildren, flowers, architecture, churches. Remember Jean? She rediscovered the beauty of life after being treated for depression. She found joy in her ministry, but as time went on, she wanted to record the beauty she found. She returned to her camera and took photography classes to capture the beauty she saw for her own appreciation and for sharing with others.

Some of us are word junkies. Others are moved by the language of music. Some are grounded in the sacred music of J. S. Bach, others in gospel music or spirituals. Music is an important part of worship and daily life. It may gently awaken us or lull us to sleep. It may help us think, or it may temporarily take us away from daily frustrations. Music connects directly to our emotions. Have you ever seen movie footage accompanied by background music and then viewed the same scenes with no musical soundtrack? The music creates an emotional backdrop and allows us to feel that we are part of the action rather than mere observers.

Music also reflects and helps define our life experiences. For people of certain generations, rock music spoke to us at a time when we were especially impressionable. The rhythm, the volume, the whine of the electric guitars, and the countercultural lyrics affected us and annoyed our parents.

Now rap or hip-hop is the language of Generation Y. The combination of music and words captures our imagination and expresses our feelings in a unique way. It also helps us to learn. Think about the alphabet song or the song about the books of the Bible. Do you find yourself humming in search of alphabetical order or in pursuit of a Scripture text? Music and words together can also be a powerful means of communication. African spirituals were sung as warning or support; anthems unite individuals toward a common goal; hymns inspire or encourage faith.

What we now know from research is that listening to or performing music stimulates the brain in ways that improve intellectual function. Music is related to improved mathematical performance and growth in reading skills. We also know that listening to music has other beneficial outcomes. Music therapy developed as a result of observations of the effect music had on the physical and mental health of veterans of World Wars I and II. Music's effect can be calming, focusing, or distracting—the last of these helpful for pain control. It has a positive effect on depressed patients and on children with developmental or behavioral problems.[1]

Music has sentimental value, reminding us of our childhood, our teenage years, our first romance, our wedding. It also has spiritual value. Hymns take us back to our early years of faith formation and connect us to the sacraments or to the church year. For many, music may provide an intimate connection to the vast universe through the magic of classical compositions, to the joy of daily life through jazz, or to the depths of emotion through the blues. Our miraculous ears, through their connections to our brain, can hear and appreciate the purity of a single note from the deepest bass to the highest pitch, as well as the complexity of massive changing chords played by many instruments. Some people have "perfect pitch" and can name the exact note being played. Others can listen and follow each instrument's lines within a complex orchestral performance. Still others simply appreciate the beauty of the sound as created by composer and as performed by band, orchestra, choir, or soloist.

My two youngest children were born in a Lutheran hospital where the nursing staff would sing a hymn at the beginning of the morning shift. It was an unexpected and magical moment for a mother with a newborn to be greeted on a new day by song. Our days might be more special if begun with song. Alone we would clear our voices and minds and sing praise for a glorious new day. With others, we would start the day in resonant harmony—a great way to lift moods and begin the day as a team. As a musician and a Christian, I find the *Moravian Daily Texts*—daily biblical texts, prayers, and hymn verses selected by Moravian clergy and laypeople published since 1731—particularly meaningful and a good way to start the day.[2] The coupling of Scripture with a hymn verse is more likely to carry me through the day, because either the words or the music may come to mind.

Just as music is an important part of our lives and the life of the church, the visual arts have been a part of worship and life forever. Cave art had multiple uses—communication, recording, and expression. As the invention of artistic tools and the development of skills to use them have increased, we have been blessed with Michelangelo's art (the Sistine Chapel, the *Pietà*), Leonardo da Vinci's *Last Supper*, and many glorious cathedrals with amazing stained-glass windows. We learn from studying works of art—about lifestyles in a different time, about uncommon individuals, about the use of color, about the fascination of detail and the interpretation of shapes and lines. We learn how to express our innermost thoughts and feelings through different artistic media. Some enjoy photography, some sketching, painting, cartooning, sculpture, interior design, or fashion design. Art is everywhere around us. We need only to see or participate in it to enrich our lives emotionally and to be inspired intellectually by the meaning behind the art.

Think about the morning sun streaming through the stained-glass windows of a church. The colors are warm and soothing or rich and inspiring. The light within the church is transformed as the sunlight is filtered by the rich hues of the glass. It is as if God's light were entering through the windows to inspire and surround us. Glass is a mysterious substance: sand heated to liquid, it is transformed by human hands by adding minerals to capture the colors of the rainbow. The fire that creates the glass seems to be captive within it, glowing hot red or cool blue, sunny yellow or deep purple. Not only are these windows sources of color and light: often they also compose pictures that tell a story. The story may be a familiar one that reminds us of words and actions. Or we may be uncertain about the story represented, so we begin to think about the possibilities, imagining who the people in the picture might be and what they are doing. With the building of churches, stained-glass windows as art began to appear, depicting Christ and various biblical scenes. Early glass artisans sought to use art to inspire others and to tell the wonderful story. The color, shape, and representation of art glass and other works of art inspire us through our emotions and engage our minds as we contemplate the meaning of what we see.

What about other senses? In Exodus 30:22-28 we read this account:

> The Lord spoke to Moses: Take the finest spices: of liquid myrrh five hundred shekels, and of sweet-smelling cinnamon half as much, that is, two hundred fifty, and two hundred fifty of aromatic cane, and five hundred of cassia—measured by the sanctuary shekel— and a hint of olive oil; and you shall make of these a sacred anointing oil blended as by the perfumer; it shall be a holy anointing oil. With it you shall anoint the tent of meeting and the ark of the covenant, and the

table and all its utensils, and the lampstand and its utensils, and the altar of incense, and the altar of burnt offering with all its utensils, and the basin with its stand; you shall consecrate them, so that they may be most holy; whatever touches them will become holy.

This is a recipe for anointing oil, explicitly for sacred use. While the fragrance of this oil could have been used as a perfume, that practice was forbidden. This special fragrance was intended to be a sign of God and God's work. Our senses are sometimes a shortcut to knowledge. The fragrance of this anointing oil must have been an immediately recognizable sign—that this was a sacred place and that these were God's chosen people.

Most of us are used to being able to integrate information fully through all five senses. As we age, our senses may become dulled by disease or by the wear and tear of daily use. We cannot hear the higher-pitched sounds, and we may have more difficulty hearing words in a noisy environment. We need reading glasses because our arms are not long enough to hold a page at the distance where our eyes can focus the words. Our vision becomes hazy with cataracts, or we begin to have difficulty seeing well at night. It is harder to distinguish the subtle tastes of food. Our fingertips, which used to be exquisitely sensitive, are calloused and clumsy. Between our failing eyes and our fingertips, threading a needle becomes an adventure. Fortunately, our brain is created in such a way that with the loss of one sense, enhancement of the other senses serves to balance the loss. Each of our senses provides us with important information for survival, for daily life, and for a full appreciation of the world around us. It is clearly in our best interest to do whatever we can to preserve those senses through nutrition, exercise, regular screening, and avoidance of risk.

Our Wonderful Brains

The brain is an incredible three-pound organ with more than 100 billion cells and connections. The front of the brain controls planning, reasoning, movement, and some speech. This frontal area is well connected to the emotional part of the brain. The sides of the brain control hearing, speech perception, and some types of memory. The cerebellum, at the base of the brain, controls balance, posture, and coordination. It takes over learned physical behaviors like driving a car or riding a bike. The top of the brain receives input from the skin, including heat, cold, pressure, pain, and the position of the body in space. It is directly related to the part of the brain that controls voluntary movement. Different parts of the brain must collaborate in speech—one part controls the facial muscles and larynx to make the sounds while another formulates meanings from words and sentences. One part supplies nouns, another verbs; a third puts them together in logical sentences.[3]

While scientists have learned much about the body and its function—they have mapped the human genome and created a mechanical heart—the brain remains a significant mystery. It is responsible for controlling the automatic functions of life—breathing, heartbeat, temperature control—as well as for defining our personality and creating our emotions. Until recently, we thought that as we aged, we steadily lost our brain cells, or neurons, without growing new cells. Now we know that in the absence of a specific disease, neurons remain healthy until our death.[4] Scientists have recently discovered that we continue to grow new brain cells into our 70s. The aging brain is quite resilient, with mental functions intact and even some advantages that form the basis for wisdom.[5] We have learned much more about the function of the brain through many types of "brain scans." We are also learning more about the impact of lifestyle on brain function. Nutrition, education, exercise, rest, and stress can all affect the brain and how it ages.

When we hear the word "intellectual," we may think of dry, esoteric lectures on topics of no interest to us. To be intellectual is to learn or understand and to have the ability to cope with new situations.[6] Using our minds fully and keeping them engaged is essential to intellectual wellness. Most of us use only a small fraction of the brain's capacity, however. We glimpse the possibilities for the full use of the human brain when we look back on the accomplishments of a few great minds such as Leonardo da Vinci, Wolfgang Amadeus Mozart, Albert Einstein, Albert Schweitzer, Marie Curie, Dietrich Bonhoeffer, Martin Luther King, Jr., Stephen Hawking, and others.

> Michael was gifted in his ability to understand and interpret other languages. That gift brought him to a deeper theological understanding and a deeper love for God. He brought that passion to his congregations, but as time went on he began to search for intellectual stimulation. He found it on his travels as he began a new study of sacred art. The combination of the visual inspiration, the historical interpretation, and the cultural context brought new inspiration to his understanding of the gospel. This was a new take on the story that he loved to tell.

For us, the goal is not to achieve what such individuals have, but to exercise the brains that we have—to stretch and reach for more than we think we can accomplish. Using our talents to have an impact on those around us requires passion and persistence. Michelangelo's painting of the ceiling of the Sistine Chapel took about four years and *The Last Judgment* six years. Think of Grandma Moses (Anna Mary Robertson Moses), who began to paint seriously in her mid-70s and sold her first painting when she was almost 80.

Whatever we accomplish may not be as visible or as lasting as these works of art, but it is just as important. My mother had one year of college before getting married. She raised five children and then started back to college part-time. While I was in medical school, she completed college, earned a master's degree in school psychology, and had a meaningful career. Others have finished degrees, raised grandchildren, started businesses, begun writing professionally, created works of art or furniture or clothing. Some have become political or social advocates, and others have started a mission congregation or volunteered for international mission work. Before you say, "I could never do something like that," remember that it is not just the skill or the capabilities of an individual, but a passion or purpose that results in artistic or other outcomes that change the world. Each of us feels passionate about something: color, shape, words, numbers, music, sounds, plants, animals, people, history, weather, rocks—all gifts from God. We need to match our passions with purpose to inspire others and to make a difference in our family, workplace, congregation, or community.

This wonderful and complex brain is not immune to disease. Recent research has given us some understanding of Alzheimer's dementia. Having this disease is an outcome many fear—to be physically alive but mentally absent. Although we don't know the cause of Alzheimer's dementia, we do know that the risk for it increases with age and, especially among those who develop the disease when they are younger, with family history. About 3 percent of men and women ages 65 to 74 have Alzheimer's, and currently nearly half of those age 85 and older may have the disease.[7] It is important to understand that this dementia is not a result of aging but a disease process. Recent research about preventing or decreasing the impact of Alzheimer's has been encouraging. Studies have shown that people with infrequent cognitive activity (or active thinking) have up to twice the risk of Alzheimer's dementia as people with frequent cognitive activity.[8] Cognitive activity may be the factor that accounts for a decreased incidence of dementia in people with higher education or in certain occupations. Also, people with early dementia have been shown to improve significantly with cognitive rehabilitation or exercises for the brain.⁹ This is encouraging news, and the future holds hope for an even greater understanding of how we can prevent or treat dementia. It is another reason to stay mentally active.

We tend to rely on external influences, such as school or work, for mental stimulation. Although aging is inevitable, we need to remember that our brains have the capacity to grow—not physically, but in usefulness. The more we use our brain, and the more we try to adapt to change or to stress our brain positively, then the more we learn, the more we create, and the more useful our brains will become. The more we keep a balance in all aspects of health, the more responsive and reactive our minds will be. We will fully use and appreciate our senses, we will seek opportunities to learn new information or new skills, and we will surprise ourselves and others with the ability to apply our minds to making this world a better place.

For Reflection

1. What is your gift of language and how do you use it to communicate effectively?
2. What music speaks to your heart and why?
3. How do you use color or shapes in your life to create a positive environment?
4. How are you stretching your brain? How are you exercising your brain regularly?
5. How has your mind surprised you recently? How can you apply it to making this world a better place?

5

God Happens at Parties
Social Health

It was his favorite phrase: "God happens at parties." Jim believed it was true. Parties were his way of attracting the nonchurched to come and experience the love of Christ expressed by the faithful community celebrating life. If the congregational event wasn't billed as a party, it became one through his sheer joy of living and sharing love. "Where one or two are gathered in his name," he would say.

This infectious joy was not always a blessing. It had been an issue in seminary with some of the professors who thought his humor reflected an attitude that was disrespectful or less than pastoral. That perception caused enough concern to raise serious questions about his fitness for public ministry. Jim never questioned his call. His enthusiasm for ministry never waned, and his happiness could never be stifled. Like a child's eagerness, it would just bubble up and spill over.

Though childlike in its pure joy, his happiness reflected a deep love of Christ and family. His sense of humor was simply his way of experiencing life. It was unusual to have a conversation with him that didn't include laughter. His romance with his wife, Martha, was as obvious after 25 years of marriage as it was when the couple were newlyweds in seminary. His love for and pride in his children was apparent through his words and actions.

Jim's early years of ministry were in rural parishes, where he became a well-loved leader in the community. His ministry grew over the years to include the work he loved—youth and mission ministries. Opportunities for parties and the parties themselves just got bigger. Along the way he made many acquaintances who would become lifetime friends. Many were envious of his passion. A few were jealous.

Isolation is a major risk factor for early death. We are social creatures with a need for love. Without love we get sick—literally. The first years of life are critical in the formation of our wellness. To lack the basic necessities of food and shelter is damaging, but when a child suffers the absence of love and of human touch, those deficits can result in a lifelong inability to love others or to receive love. When we have experienced love, living with the loss of a loved one makes us vulnerable physically and emotionally. Just as we need to assure a supply of healthful food and water, shelter from the elements, adequate rest, and spiritual renewal, we must nurture relationships throughout life to ensure a social safety net to surround us when we need it.

Social Networks

I asked my young-adult son for ideas on what to include in this chapter about social health for adults preparing for retirement. Sometimes wisdom comes from unexpected places. He said, "They need to have a social network, and they need to have it before they retire." He went on observe that many pastors aren't very good at developing or maintaining a social network during their ministry because of all the demands on their time. He suggested that clergy reach outside "the church" and join a classic car club or a bikers' club. He added that it was essential after retirement also to maintain social contact within the church—returning to seminary for classes or being an active member in another congregation.

I am sure that his wise observations come from living with his pastor dad, but I think the passion in his answer came from living with a similar transition—from college student to young adult. Social networks are essential. They keep us emotionally healthy and physically and intellectually productive. They help us to continue to define who we are. Our identity is complex. At some stages of life, occupational identity seems to take priority, but if our self-identity or social identity is left to languish, we experience an identity crisis at retirement. In American culture, adults are defined by occupation. When we are introduced to new people, the next question is likely to be, "And what do you do?" As professionals, we have uniforms by which others can recognize our identity without asking. For physicians it is the white coat. For clergy in some church traditions, it is the clerical collar. I often wonder about colleagues who are always "in uniform." There are important reasons for wearing clerical garb, but I am concerned for those who are not comfortable without it. If your identity and social function are defined entirely by your occupation, you will find a gaping hole in retirement, or a resistance to leaving an occupation when the time is right.

As human beings, we are always seeking our place in the world. As children, we find our place within the family. As we grow and go off to school, we begin to understand and to develop our place in a larger community. We are the "good student," "good musician," "class clown," "popular student," or "star athlete." Then we leave school and take our place as parent and homemaker, teacher, coach, pastor, doctor, salesperson, or chef. As we mature, we are able to balance several identities or roles because we have learned how to be a student, worker, parent, friend, or relative. Problems arise when we are unable to keep a sense of balance by understanding the multiple roles and identities we have as adults. We are familiar with many whose jobs consume their identity; the result can be tragic—depression or suicide when a business fails;

divorce or dysfunctional relationships with spouses or children; vulnerability to alcohol or drug abuse or other addictive behaviors.

Occupational and family roles can be so energy-consuming for many of us that they leave little time or desire to seek out other social activities. Unfortunately, the demands of those roles may also leave us unsatisfied or unfulfilled. If we are unable to use other gifts, learn new skills, or make new relationships, our health suffers. If we are physically exhausted, intellectually stifled, or emotionally frazzled, we aren't able to be the best parent or worker. Being active in other social networks enlarges our community and reminds us that we are also students, hobbyists, athletes or sports enthusiasts, musicians, gardeners, or collectors. These activities allow us to express ourselves in other ways and to use gifts that bring us happiness and may bring joy to others. A change of scenery and conversation and a use of different skills can be energizing.

> Jim's love of parties reflected his extroversion and the self-affirmation he received from the attention of others and the reflection of others' happiness when all were having fun. Some may have interpreted this partying style as superficial, but the message was always clear. Jim's love of life came from his love of God, and whether one was an active church member or someone who had never set foot in a church, this love was contagious. His influence was important in leading some to Christ and in creating social networks that had fun, had a purpose, and spread the gospel story.

Being active in a congregation reminds us that we belong to a fellowship of believers with a mission to do the work of Christ in this world. This essential connection reminds us that the needs of the world are beyond our own homes or workplaces. Studies have shown that active involvement in church results in better health and longevity. Several explanations are offered, including the well-known value of social support. This support is emotional (protecting against depression and anxiety), physical (encouraging a healthy lifestyle), and vocational (giving a sense of purpose). A congregation is also the place where spirituality is inspired, nourished, and renewed to carry us through daily life.

When these social networks haven't been nourished, the changes of the third age can be difficult. Children grow up and leave home. When most of your energy and time have been spent on the needs and in the company of the children, suddenly you need to find new things to do and new people to be with. Parents age and become disabled. If those relationships haven't been nurtured, the stress of meeting the needs of those who used to take care of you may result in a breakdown of those relationships or of your own health. You may need to change jobs or calls or appointments, or you may consider retirement. Those social networks that were a part of work— your staff, your peers, your congregation—are lost or changed. The unhealthy response to this change is to cling to the social networks you were a part of before your retirement.

Continuing to participate in the church you served as a pastor is difficult, for you and for the congregation (as well as for the new pastor) when members continue to see you as their pastor. Continuing to meet with colleagues who remain in ministry in the same community may not work. Your personal needs and experiences are different because your lives are now on different paths. On the other hand, being without a social network, particularly if your spouse or partner continues to work, leaves you without social interaction and without productive activities. As a consequence, you may feel resentment toward your partner or make unreasonable demands on his or her time to meet your needs. Worse yet, a lack of social connections may make it all too easy for you to turn into a couch potato—an outcome detrimental not only to social but also to physical, emotional, intellectual, vocational, and spiritual health.

Successful retirement means the formation of new social networks that also meet physical, emotional, intellectual, vocational or spiritual needs. Continuing with relationships from your occupation is good if you have other things in common outside of work and if the purpose of those social activities goes beyond work-related topics. Finding new avenues to develop new friends is an important effort that should start in anticipation of retirement. The best situation is one in which you are eager for retirement because you have so many other activities going on.

> After retirement, Jim began collecting antique toys. Whether it was to make up for a childhood with very few toys or an excuse to continue playing with toys, no one was sure. The beauty of this hobby was that in addition to the fun of discovering new toys, each with its own story, Jim began to use the toys as a new ministry. He brought a few of his toys along when invited to speak about his faith to various groups. He discovered that it was a great way to connect with audiences of all ages. Everyone has a favorite toy that evokes happy memories. Sharing these stories with others was a way to share the joy of the gospel.

Friendship

Some people have the special gift of making friends. Jim can go hardly anywhere in the country without being recognized and greeted warmly. When he finds such a place, he makes a friend of a stranger. For some people, making friends and being a memorable and admired personality may come easily, while forming true and deep friendship is another matter entirely. Whether you are introverted or extroverted, the number of lifelong or deeply trusted friends is few. Jim is an extrovert whose energy comes from being with other people. Extroverts think by talking, glow with energy, and engage in many activities. They are often restless when alone. Introverts lose personal energy in the company of others. They need time alone to recharge their batteries. They prefer one-on-one conversations and think carefully before they speak. Most of us have qualities of both extroversion and introversion but tend to lean more toward one or the other quality.

We cannot be truly whole without the dimension that friends bring to our lives. We understand our personhood through sharing what is most important and valuable with friends. We see ourselves reflected in their eyes, and we learn to understand another almost as well as we come to understand ourselves. Friends are sounding posts to talk about many issues that become real and personal through ongoing conversations. Friends are mirrors that reflect reality—pretty or ugly. They instinctively know when they are needed and what to say or do. Friends recognize emotions that are misinterpreted by others and allow them to be expressed. They know our history, family, successes, and failures. Life continually changes around us, but our friends keep us grounded. Friends know us as we really are—not as the pastor, administrator, counselor, child, parent, teacher, coach, or boss.

Friends deserve time and attention. Even when connections run deep, the closest friendships can fall apart without attention. We read stories about friends from college who get together to celebrate their friendship every year for decades. You know what these experiences are like—recounting stories from the past, laughing and crying, catching up on family details, complaining about bodily and other changes. Reunions give us an opportunity to renew relationships with friends and relatives, to give and get updates on the changes in our lives. Nurturing special friendships means setting aside time on a regular basis to meet, enjoy activities together, or spend time talking about things that matter. Regular phone calls, e-mails, or letters to friends who live far away can keep the closeness that is easily rekindled when you can see each other again. Keeping a regular "night out" with a local friend or friends reserves a time to relax, laugh, cry, or just stay connected. Friends are an invaluable resource when you are trying to change lifestyle behaviors or learn new skills. You are much more likely to succeed at increasing your level of physical activity if you do something with a friend—go for regular walks or bike rides, play tennis or golf, join a basketball league.

> Jim has one sister who lives across the continent. Although their lives have been very different, he has made a point of writing regularly and seeing her every year. He knows the importance of sharing childhood memories, laughing about the many entertaining family stories, sharing pictures of loved ones, and just being close. There is a limit to how long they can be together without getting on each other's nerves, but neither of them would have it any other way.

For pastors, the issue of friendships has become more complex. Data from a 2001 survey from the Evangelical Lutheran Church in America indicated that 23 percent of clergy reported a serious problem with friends in the past 12 months. In my travels across the United States, speaking to pastors about health and wellness, I asked what they thought that statistic indicated. One young man made a telling statement: "We don't have any friends." The issues of sexual abuse and impropriety in clergy have resulted in discussions of boundaries and may be one of several barriers to the development of healthy friendships. The lack of social invitations in a world that retreats to the comforts of nesting at home, and the need to be politically appropriate—these stunt the growth of relationships. In the reality of the unending demands of public ministry, the development of new friendships and the nurture of old ones are lost. Retirement can be a time of rekindling and rejoicing in relationships. Certainly new friendships are made in retirement, but if we haven't been socially active during our working life, our social skills may be pretty stiff in retirement. Friends are life-sustaining as we age. They can literally be of help meeting daily needs through transportation, shopping for groceries, taking us to doctor's appointments. The value of relationships goes beyond the practical, however. We know that isolation can be fatal because of many studies that have shown that individuals who are isolated or disconnected from others are at increased risk (two to three times) for dying prematurely.[1] What protective effects do social networks provide? One concept is that of *buffering*. Relationships help to buffer the effects of stressful times and life transitions. Another is the likelihood that relationships will help to promote healthy behaviors—being active, eating regularly and more nutritionally, avoiding cigarettes or the abuse of alcohol. Studies have even shown that lonely people, although they sleep as many hours as those who are not lonely, experience poorer-quality sleep. Other studies have shown that loneliness has a detrimental effect on blood pressure and on the immune system that fights infections. As we age, it may be difficult to sustain friendships because of poor health, lack of transportation, and the loss of friends to death or illness. Creating and sustaining our social networks has to be a lifetime effort. The church can be a particularly beneficial network because of its mission to support and reach out to its own membership and to others in need.

Love and Intimacy

Until death parts us, we have a need for intimacy—to know another person almost as we know ourselves and to share the most personal experiences without reservation. Intimate relationships continue even beyond the grave because of the significance of the memories shared. To feel loved completely, with all one's flaws and failures, makes life meaningful. It fills in the cracks of our incompleteness and encourages and inspires us to go beyond where we would venture alone. Some people have enjoyed this gift of intimacy for decades, others for years. Some have had a glimpse but no more.

We can experience intimacy in a variety of realms. We share both emotional and physical intimacies. In our families, we experience intimacy when we witness birth and death and other private, life-changing and sometimes earth-shattering transitions—joyous and tragic moments when family members comfort or celebrate with us. We can even share intimacy with strangers by the virtue of circumstances—war, accidents, desperate need, or unexpected events—that create indelible memories and lifelong bonds. Parent and child, or caretaker and care-receiver, become intimate as daily needs that cannot be accomplished alone need assistance. The depth of love in these intimate situations is indescribable—passionate, nurturing, selfless, undeniable, unquenchable. We all need someone we can trust completely to share our deepest personal needs and desires, even in our darkest hour or greatest need.

If we have known this love, then we can glimpse the even more profound reality of the love God has for us. We are not alone. We are loved as children of God, and we are saved through the love of God, who sacrificed his own son for our souls. This is the foundation upon which we build our lives—the trust that allows us to risk our own safety or comfort to share the love of God with others through word and deed. This love guides our lives—as we raise our families and work in our communities. If we know this love, then we are able to see the need in others. Sometimes the need is in our own families—children feeling unloved, family members struggling with depression or disease, individuals fearing loss of a loved one or of a job. Sometimes the need is in our community—people dying alone or fighting cancer or AIDS, people finding themselves homeless or dealing with mental illness, people who have become violent because of abuse and unresolved anger, people who struggle to learn the language and the ways of a new home country.

Our need for love never ends. In middle age, we have probably experienced the love of parents, partners, or children, and during this time their need for us may not be as great. This may be a time to use our energies to share the love we have experienced with those who are in need—members of our community who are homeless, without sufficient food or clothing, or without parental nurturing. Being a pastor means sharing God's love with others in need, but the energy to do this day after day comes from replenishing one's own need for love—from spouse, family, and friends.

Community Involvement

Did you know that volunteers live longer? This statement doesn't necessarily apply to volunteering on the board of the symphony or doing someone's taxes (although those are good things to do). More beneficial is the kind of face-to-face volunteering in which you can experience the emotions and the connection of doing work for, bringing food to, or spending time with someone in need. Harold Koenig, physician and director of Duke University's Center for the Study of Religion/ Spirituality and Health writes:

> Deciding to give time, talents, and kindness to others by volunteering is an action fully under a person's control. Realizing that everyone right now has the power to change his or her life and the lives of others toward well-being and health is empowering. What matters is not how big your gifts and abilities are, but rather that you use them to make life better for others. It's all about being faithful with whatever gifts you have, large or small—because the power comes from the purpose behind the actions, not from the results.[2]

It is that sense of purpose, in addition to the emotional lift received from physically helping others, that brings balance to the Wholeness Wheel (see page 5). We have learned that receiving love is essential if one is to thrive, but giving love is equally important. Giving out of a love for Christ and for God's people, without expecting anything in return, brings us vocational fulfillment and spiritual inspiration. Being with others engaged in the same activities and learning about those whose needs are being met enhances our social health. It is particularly health-giving to learn to understand and spend time with others whose circumstances, culture, language, or religion is different from our own.

Caring for the aged will be an important social issue and ministry in the coming decades. In the United States, the number of people over age 65 is predicted to double from 2000 to 2030. We will need to redesign living arrangements, health-care services, public transportation, and other support services to meet the needs of this growing population. While individual financial, medical, or basic daily-living concerns will need to be addressed, older adults will also have vocational needs. Developing meaningful outlets for the increasing numbers of relatively healthy retired people will require creativity and organization. For example, communities might develop community centers near senior housing to ensure that basic shopping and health-care services are accessible and that educational offerings, artistic opportunities, and volunteer options are encouraged and readily available.

Leave a Legacy

We are born and raised in the social context of family. We spend our adult lives creating our own family or network of friends and relatives and working in other social networks. We gain self-esteem through the love and respect of others. As we near the end of life, we have a need to be remembered or to leave a mark on the world we inhabited. We may leave a legacy through the memories of our loved ones or through more tangible evidence. One specific way of accomplishing a lasting legacy is through an ethical will. Barry Baines, a family physician in hospice and palliative care, explains, "Ethical wills are used for recording and sharing values, beliefs, life's lessons, hopes for the future and love and forgiveness with family, friends and community."[3] An ancient tradition going back to biblical days, ethical wills eventually took the form of written documents that often accompanied legal wills. An ethical will is a unique document—reflecting its author's life history, private thoughts, and hopes for the future. Writing an ethical will is a gift to those left behind, but it is also a gift to the writer. It brings reassurance that what is important to the writer has been communicated. It is also a learning process for the author, who discovers what feelings and values are meaningful and necessary to communicate. Preparing an ethical will brings peace of mind that, regardless of the amount or quality of time you have left to spend with loved ones, you have recorded a message of love and reassurance for those left behind.

In addition to ethical wills, we can pass on to our loved ones many other lasting, tangible representations of our life—photographs, art work, letters, published materials, quilts, hand-made clothing or furniture, perennial gardens. We can also leave vocational legacies—public histories of accomplishments, buildings, charitable gifts or foundations, public policy or legislation, healthy congregations, mission work, or students who go on to serve well.

You may want to leave a personal message or music for children or other loved ones in writing, pictures, video, or audiotape. You may want to create gifts for special family members or friends—scrapbooks, quilts, artwork, or stories. Jim began collecting antique toys as an enjoyable hobby and an extension of his ministry outreach. He also started carving toys and other decorations as gifts for family and friends as an outlet for his creativity and time. These personal creations are cherished by those who receive them. They bring a lasting memory of someone special in their lives. Although someone living with a terminal illness might find it particularly important to create such messages or gifts for loves ones, the task can be just as meaningful for those who are healthy and active. Pastors may have stories, meditations, sermons, or prayers that have been meaningful in their ministry that they want to leave with family or friends. Ministry is also a wonderful opportunity to help others prepare and leave a meaningful legacy.

We know that our lives, from infancy to the end of life, have meaning because of the people that surround us. From the first awareness of facial expressions and the excitement of vocalizing to the last words or eye contact with a loved one, we know the power of social connections. While they may at times be difficult or take time to sustain, these social connections are essential to our health.

For Reflection

1. Think about your closest friendships. How are you nurturing those relationships? How are you seeking out new friendships?
2. Are you an introvert or an extrovert? How do you recharge your batteries?
3. Intimacy is essential. How are your needs for intimacy being met?
4. What are your social networks? How do they keep you healthy?
5. What is the legacy you would like to leave, and how will you do that?
6. How are you actively connected with your community? What gifts do you have to contribute to improve community life?

6

Follow Your Passion
Vocational Health

George spent his whole life in human services. He was ordained but served only a few years in a parish. He was well known for his work with the homeless, having written several books about his experiences. He spent the last 10 years of his career traveling, giving seminars and presentations. When he turned 60, he and his wife, Marion, decided to move back to the area where they grew up. Having lived in several cities over the years, he really wanted to get back to a rural setting where he could live affordably but own more land.

One of his dreams was to have a flower garden. Marion was good at arranging fresh flowers and enjoyed drying flowers for decorating. The first two years they planned their garden space and began to prepare the soil. During that time they studied together the natural wild flowers and perennials that thrived in the area. The third year they began to plant. By the end of the fifth year they were surrounded by beauty throughout the growing season and were busy from April through October with work in the garden.

Late in the summer and during the fall, Marion was occupied with drying flowers and making arrangements. George began to look for something else. Years ago, he had taken a woodworking class and had really enjoyed it. He began picking up pieces of wood from the property and from the shed. He invested in a few tools to begin in earnest and attended a community woodworking class. Eventually he needed to have a big project for his class. George had loved his work with people who were homeless—counseling them, helping them with food and shelter needs, arranging for needed health care and mental health services, helping them deal with addictions. But the one thing that continued to haunt him was the lack of dignity they were afforded in death. He had seen many individuals die—most prematurely from drugs, alcohol, violence, or exposure. Many just disappeared into the county system, buried without any acknowledgment in a shabby wooden box. Homeless during life, they were finally laid to rest in a manner little different from the treatment they had received during their anonymous and difficult lives.

He contrasted these experiences with the funerals at which he had officiated. Much time, energy, and negotiation was devoted to the discussion of what type of casket, liner, and vault the deceased would have wanted. Often more time was spent on this decision than on the service of remembrance. George had no doubts about eternal life and had little fear of death, but he had an idea about easing the transition. He would use his woodworking skills to create his own coffin. He selected the wood thoughtfully, considering hardness, durability, and ease of carving. He bought his wood and began the project built to his measurements and weight. It took him three months to finish. When it was complete, he was proud of his work. He decided to add temporary shelves and use it as a bookshelf. He placed it upright in his study and filled the coffin with his favorite books and memorabilia.

He proudly displayed his work to friends and neighbors. Many expressed an interest and asked George if he was thinking of making more. Eventually he realized that he could enjoy his hobby and bring the same joy and peace to others that he felt in having made this simple preparation for death. He began to take orders and found that building the coffins was only a part of his work. The discussions he had with his customers about their lives, their faith, and their plans for their deaths enriched his life immeasurably. He made new friends of all ages and used his gifts of listening and reflecting to help them prepare for the inevitable— spiritually, physically, and emotionally. What was a hobby became a ministry to his community.

Use Your Gifts

Our gifts are many. We need to recognize and develop them. We tend to spend the young-adult years deciding where to apply ourselves in vocation and then discovering what our gifts are. Sometimes we find that we are in the wrong place, situated in an occupation for which we don't have gifts or that we don't enjoy because it uses skills that don't come easily. Even if we do find an occupation for which we have the gifts, we are often out of balance—using one gift and letting others languish. Some are lucky enough to find a vocation in midlife that makes full use of several gifts—a satisfying situation.

George directed his gifts in ministry toward a special population—the homeless. He drew on his love for God and for others and on his communication and organizational skills to make their lives better. He learned how to speak publicly for the purpose of raising awareness and raising money for his ministry and the ongoing care of the homeless. His was an itinerant ministry—his church was on the streets and in many different homeless shelters over the years. Living for so many years with those whose belongings were in plastic bags, knapsacks, or grocery carts, he recognized the longing to go home and to create a seasonal environment that surrounded him and Marion in beauty and comfort. Finally, using his hands in a newly developed skill brought his ministry full circle to provide final resting homes for others and eventually for himself. It was a grounding—using his hands to provide food, warmth, blessings, love, and shelter.

Sometimes it is not how we are able to use the gifts we have been given, but whether we find ourselves in an environment that sustains us. We may know that we are in a vocation in which we can make a significant difference, but we may be losing energy because something is missing for our own growth or sustenance. My father was a social worker for many years and loved his work. As his tenure and experience increased, he found himself in positions of leadership. As rewarding as that may have been—in making a difference in many people's lives and working with people that he respected and admired— he was missing the face-to-face contact with those who needed his help. In search of some "grounding," he decided to drive a sugar-beet truck during harvest season all through the night. When I asked why he would do such a crazy thing, he said something about the smell of the dirt—a comment that made little sense to a teenager. He finished his career in the organization he had once led, with a contract that specified no meetings or unimportant paperwork. He hit the rural roads of North Dakota, counseling patients as he loved to do.

Follow Your Passion

A passion is a burning desire or conviction, a source of energy that drives you to do something. The passion for ministry grows from being called to bring your gifts, energy, and love of Christ to serve others in Christ's name. Regardless of vocation, the road to success in having an impact on your community is to love what you do. If you love the mystery of science and the opportunity to bring health and healing to individuals with disease or suffering, you may choose to be a physician or health-care provider. If you love to bring beauty to enrich the lives of others, you might be an artist or musician; if you love to communicate the truths about the world, a journalist or a creative writer.

George's lifelong passion was to bring a sense of home to the homeless. Food, shelter, comfort, and identity are essential realities of home that sustain us in our daily lives. George was raised in a loving and grounded Christian home, and his call was to work hard to provide for others who may not have had that strong foundation or who had lost it along the way. As his expertise and his reputation grew, he found himself totally removed from the people he served and often absent from his own home. In his retirement he needed to rekindle that passion by re-establishing his sense of home. Working with his hands, gardening, and then woodworking provided another way of grounding himself. Being at home awakened his passion. Many fear the unknown transition in death from this life to eternal life as a type of homelessness. Creating his coffin with his own hands gave George a sense of peace. As his friends began to request their own coffins, George realized that it wasn't just the gift of a hand-crafted box but the gift of peace and comfort that he could provide for others.

You may have lost your passion along the way with life's demands. Take some time to rediscover that passion or to rekindle a passion whose flame has grown dim. It may be a passion for learning, for art or music, for helping children grow and develop, for numbers, for poetry, or for prayer and devotion.

We often associate passion with the heart. Heart attacks are life-changing crises in the lives of many middle-aged folk. One of the warning signs of a heart attack is something called "vital exhaustion." It is defined by the Institute of Medicine's "Health and Behavior" report as excessive fatigue, increased irritability, and demoralization.[1] We think that heart disease is the result of poor diet, smoking, being overweight, high cholesterol causing sludge in our arteries, and high blood pressure putting stress on the heart. What we forget is the direct but somewhat mysterious relationship between emotions, heart disease, and death. Terry Hershey describes it in a different way: "We church folks were encouraged to burn ourselves out for God—conjuring images of one so weary with well doing he begins to smolder at the collar and eventually spontaneously combusts, to perpetual sainthood."[2]

Many of us, by the time we are middle-aged, have felt vital exhaustion. Certainly in human services, in health care, and in the church, many of us give of ourselves until we can't give anymore. We become exhausted, dragging ourselves out of bed and off to work. We struggle to stay awake, to listen, and to care about what we are doing. We become irritable, reacting to simple requests with inappropriate anger or frustration. We question our ability, our sanity, and our reasoning in choosing such a vocation. Hearts that were full of love for others, compassion, and caring become depleted and fragile.

A passion can become a burden or consume us in a form of spontaneous combustion. While passion for vocation is part of a joyful life, passion without boundaries or without balance can become fatal—physically or vocationally. If that is the case in your life, it is time to seek balance, rest, and renewal so that you can find your passion and direct it in a healthier way.

Search for Wholeness

Middle age is a time when we search for a way to make ourselves whole again. We become aware of what may be missing in our lives and of what is truly important. It is an opportunity to plan for a life that creates greater balance. It may mean changing jobs, moving to a home that doesn't demand as much attention, moving closer to family, or rearranging commitments to spend more time with those we love. It may mean going back to school or reacquainting ourselves with a favorite avocation long ignored.

It may mean paying more attention to our physical or emotional health. We spend much of our adult life giving of ourselves to our jobs and to our family. Important as that may be, our own health cannot go unattended without our facing serious health issues and loss of the ability to work or care for others. Take the time to assess the state of your physical health. What about that 40 pounds you put on over the past 30 years? What about your blood pressure or your cholesterol? Are you eating well, sleeping well, physically active? What about your mood? Is it healthy and positive? Do you have the energy you need to do what needs to be done, with some left over for fun? These are vocational issues. If joy in life and life satisfaction are a result of meaningful vocation in the context of loving family and a community of believers, then physical and emotional health are essential ingredients.

Take an inventory of your life to date. What has made you most happy? What are you most proud of? What have you overlooked that needs your attention? How have you lived your life as a Christian? As a child? As a parent? As a minister? As a community member? What are your dreams? What goals have you not yet achieved? What kind of legacy do you want to leave behind?

Now is the time. You have the maturity, knowledge, and experience to make this a serious endeavor. You are capable of assessing your current reality and of making changes toward wholeness. Your current vocation may be coming to a close, or you may be in transition to a new form of that vocation.

While pastors have been in ministry to others and have helped to lead a congregation in its mission in ministry, these acts of ministry may not bring the same sense of fulfillment or inspiration. The third age may bring the time and the opportunity for personal acts of service that are more palpable or meaningful or that reach a different population or meet different needs.

Your family is probably making some significant transitions—parents or other family members are experiencing serious illness; some may have died. Children or others are starting out on their own vocational paths. It's time to care for yourself and to plan for the future.

What About Purpose?

Planning for the future suggests purpose. Retirement may be the end of a particular occupational or vocational phase, but it is the beginning of another. Planning means having objectives and goals. One plan might be to travel to see all 50 United States and to learn American history as you go, connecting with as many family members as you can find and taking photographs or writing a journal about your journey. Another plan might be to volunteer at a cancer center or hospice to listen and learn about others' journeys and to help them meet their final goals, learning what it means to be acutely or terminally ill or dying. A third might be to volunteer to help new Americans make the transition to living in the United States by offering time and skills to teach English as a second language, how to drive, how to shop for groceries, and how to cook new foods—while at the same time you are learning about their culture, language, religion, and cuisine.

You may have plans and goals for your home—to make it accessible for handicapped people, to freshen it up and sell it so that you can move to another location or to a lower-maintenance home. Search for your family heritage by researching documents online or in person or by traveling to your country of origin and interviewing other relatives or neighbors. Prepare a timeline and story for your descendants as a gift for the future. You may be needed to help raise grandchildren or other relatives and may need to adapt your home or create a play space for a younger generation. You may choose to return to school, not as a student but as a teacher. If you have developed special gifts in your ministry or vocation, you may be needed to teach those practical aspects to the next generation of pastors, church workers, and other community-service people. Get involved with local, state, or national politics or community organization by canvassing, serving on committees or boards, volunteering in campaigns or community-service projects, or raising funds. You'll meet new people while making your community a better place. Serve your college, seminary, or public school by teaching, organizing service projects, sitting on boards or committees, or volunteering on campus and reconnecting with students and with your own history. If you love to be outdoors, volunteer to tend a public or private garden, to mow lawns, shovel snow, or tend naturalized prairie or wetlands to get exercise and to enjoy the beauty of the seasons and the company of those who love the land. Take cooking lessons and plan to entertain your family and friends regularly while trying out new recipes—or bring your culinary skills and your love of cooking to bear on serving meals to the elderly or to the homeless, meeting their needs while learning their stories. Join with other friends and start a food pantry in your community. See that the shelves are stocked with healthy foods; make the project also a source for warm clothing, blankets, or used books.

For Reflection

1. What are your gifts? How are you using them? Which ones would you like to encourage or develop more fully?
2. What is your passion in life? What do you feel driven to do? How will that change in retirement?

3. Are you in balance? What are you thinking about giving up or cutting back on, and where do you want to grow?
4. What is the purpose for this time of your life? Do you share that purpose with someone else? How are you planning toward that purpose?

7

Faith and Life
Spiritual Health

The Wholeness Wheel (see page 5) illustrates the importance of spirituality to health. We are created by God, and through baptism we are new creations in Christ and members of the body of Christ. While the dimensions of health are related and necessary to good health, spiritual health is what surrounds and protects the other dimensions of health. The original Wholeness Wheel developed by the InterLutheran Coordinating Committee on Ministerial Health and Wellness has an outer circle defined as "faith-hardiness." This concept is described more fully by Gary Harbaugh, professor in pastoral care and pastoral staff for Lutheran Disaster Response, in *The Confident Christian*.[1] Hardiness is a psychological term, defined as a resilience to stress and trauma. Faith hardiness is that resilience to stress and trauma experienced by Christians as a result of their confident knowledge that God is ever-present in our lives. When we are certain of that presence, it is as if we were toddlers again—venturing out bravely on our own, trying new activities and reaching out to new people, knowing that the parent we love and trust implicitly is right there. We are less likely to experience lasting fear or anxiety, less likely to feel depressed or hopeless when we are in active conversation and in daily relationship with God.

As a young woman, Ellen worked as a part-time youth director in a church close to the college campus. She enjoyed the sense of community with all ages and delighted in the joy she saw in the faces of the youth as they were singing, talking, or praying. It was a special time—not just for making friends, but for exploring her own faith. She found that teaching and walking with others in their faith journey was a challenge for her personal faith. She also began to think about going to seminary and seeking ordination as a parish pastor.

Although Ellen's father was a retired pastor, this was the first time she had considered public ministry as a vocation or calling. She began to pray about her decision—at first reflecting with God on her journey to this point and then more specifically asking for guidance and clarity. "Lord, show me the way" became her daily prayer.

She also began to meet regularly with her pastor. They discussed theology, the joys and frustrations of public ministry, the congregation's mission, and issues of personal faith. He listened, and they prayed together. He began to lead her on a journey of discovery, asking about her relationship with God, her prayer life, her values, her coping mechanisms, what gave her joy and what gave her pain. They talked about her mentors and role models and began to look into the future. He helped her establish time in her day for devotional study and for prayer.

Years later—after seminary, marriage, and children, and in the third year of her second call—she began to have doubts about her calling to ordained ministry. She was exhausted and somewhat frustrated with the senior pastor of the congregation she served, with the daily grind and the constant swirl of what seemed to be petty issues and disagreements. She talked to her husband and to her peers. Someone suggested she seek out a spiritual director. She immediately thought back to her experience with her pastor when she was a college student and the renewal and revitalization that she had experienced through that relationship. She realized that she was spiritually running on empty and needed to refuel.

Research on the health of clergy published in 1980 may have illustrated this concept of faith hardiness. A study that followed a group of Protestant clergymen for 10 years found that they had a lower death rate for most causes of death when compared with physicians, lawyers, and other European-American males of the same age.[2] Unfortunately, another study published almost 20 years later showed that clergy were among the top 10 occupations to suffer death from heart disease.[3] Faith hardiness may have come up against other stresses and cultural changes that neutralized or overcame that resilience.

Faith and Health

Health-care practitioners have just "discovered" the impact of spirituality on health. Healers have always known the power of belief and the mystery of the human body. As medicine has become a field of scientific study and health care has become a menu of pharmacological or technological fixes, health-care providers have come to believe more in their own powers or the powers of science. Most physicians who have practiced for several years have experienced the unexplainable, however. Some of them turned their attention toward the power of prayer and religion and its effect on health and disease. Decades of studies have been reviewed and summarized by recent authors. The findings are rather striking and include:

- People who regularly attend religious services have lower rates of illness and death than do infrequent attenders or nonattenders.

- People who report a religious affiliation have lower rates of heart disease, cancer, and high blood pressure.

- Older adults who participate in private and congregational religious activities have fewer symptoms, less disability, and lower rates of depression, anxiety and dementia.

- Religious participation is the strongest determinant of psychological well-being in African Americans.

- Actively religious people live longer, on average, than the nonreligious.[4]

What is link between faith and health? Dr. Harold Koenig, director of the Duke University Center for the Study of Religion/Spirituality and Health, has participated in and compiled the results of many studies on the link between faith and health. Studies have found two ways religion directly benefits health. First, respect for the body is encouraged by a social support system, including a strong marriage and participation in a loving congregation. Involvement in such a support system results in seeking care and getting diagnosed earlier, active involvement in treatment, and following caregivers' instructions. Second, religious individuals lead healthier lifestyles by avoiding cigarettes and the abuse of drugs and alcohol as well as risky sexual behavior that can result in diseases.[5]

There are indirect benefits as well.[6] The social and emotional support of being actively involved in a congregation and sharing the bonds of faith buffer the impact of stress and decrease depression and anxiety. The hormonal impact of chronic stress or depression can lead to high blood pressure, heart disease, and weakening of the immune system that can lead to infections, cancer, heart attacks, and stroke. Studies have shown that religious individuals have less depression and recover from depression more quickly; they are protected from suicide and have lower blood pressures and a lower risk of heart attack.

Why, then, is the health of our church leaders declining? What does that finding mean for clergy or other church workers as they plan for retirement? Can it be that tending and nurturing the faith and spirituality of others leaves little or no time to nurture one's own faith? Have the daily demands of preparing the bulletin, planning worship services, attending staff and committee meetings, writing reports and newsletter columns, visiting the sick, counseling the troubled, preaching, teaching, and providing the sacraments whittled away at the health benefits that derive from a personal relationship with God and with a community of faith? Regardless of vocation or stage in life, experiencing the healing power of faith requires an active personal faith.

Faith Hardiness

How do we cultivate an active personal faith that helps to develop faith hardiness? Dr. Koenig has some ideas based on years of experience in caring for and studying faithful people. For those who are already religious, including church leaders, active and retired, he suggests:

1. Attend church more frequently, become more involved in your congregation, join a prayer group, or reach out spiritually to others in need.
2. Identify your special talents and use them to help the less fortunate people in your church or community.
3. Attend a prayer or Scripture study group regularly.
4. Set aside time each morning for prayer.
5. Pray with your family each day.
6. Discuss religious topics with friends and family.
7. Read religious scriptures or inspirational literature every day.

8. Before making major decisions, pray about them and listen for an answer.
9. Discuss with a trusted clergy leader your feelings and thoughts about God.
10. Act consistently with your religious principles, reaching out to others of different faiths, socioeconomic situations, or cultures.[7]

An active faith is not just the acknowledgment that you were "born" Lutheran or Catholic or Baptist or Methodist. You can't assume that being a pastor or lay leader in a church means that you have an active faith. You can't even trust that by practicing the outward acts of religious involvement you will become spiritually healthy. On the contrary, studies have shown that extrinsic religion—active involvement in church activities for extrinsic reasons such as social status rather than as a result of a deep personal faith—actually has a negative correlation to measures of health.[8]

An active personal faith involves living out daily your beliefs through a personal relationship with God. Living in faith means reading, studying, and singing the Word of God. It involves praying silently and aloud, specifically and meditatively, using someone else's words or your own, in joy and thankfulness or sorrow, pain or frustration. Living faithfully means sharing your beliefs and your love of God through word and action with family, friends, coworkers, and community. It means trying to use your gifts to honor God and to have a positive and lasting impact on the people and the community around you.

For those who have chosen public ministry as a vocation and as an expression of their faith, living an active personal faith becomes even more of a challenge. It becomes easy to view faith as a business and the pastor as a leader or expert or manager. Being "in charge" of faith formation and expression for a congregation can overtake the time needed to grow an active personal faith. Faith practiced as part of a job description becomes a source of stress or a vulnerability rather than a way of developing hardiness. For those pastors who may have burned out on the endless expectations of the job of ministry, retirement may represent an opportunity to escape from "church."

> As Ellen was discerning her vocation, she was in active conversation—with God, her pastor, her father, and others. Those conversations carried her through years of public ministry, but the business of life and work distracted her from that journey. She lost track of the importance of nurturing her own faith and of having meaningful personal conversations with God and with others on that journey. She had moments of questioning her call and her ability to continue in ministry. Although she was helping others along that journey, she knew she needed her own personal time to reflect, to share her own thoughts and feelings, and to seek comfort and guidance.

Worship

The weekly demands of preparation and performance in worship cannot substitute for the deep personal need for private prayer, devotion, contemplation, or participation in meaningful worship. To maintain spiritual health and build up faith hardiness, pastors also need to worship. Actively participating in meaningful worship can be a struggle when the temptation is to compare or anticipate or critique. Finding the opportunity while in public ministry is a challenge, outside of periodic leadership retreats or conferences. Retiring from a role in public ministry can be a difficult adjustment to find the proper "pew perspective" as a faithful and active member of a congregation rather than as a leader. Finding opportunities for worship and the right congregation is essential. Discovering your role in sharing your gifts and time as a member is important. This may take some exploration and some conversation with God, friends, family, and others.

As a culture, we expect comfort and convenience, and we want to expend the least possible energy. We expect mass-produced, affordable, individualized products to meet our every need. Everything is designed to appeal to our desires and needs—breakfast food, fast food, name-brand clothing, cars, job descriptions, academic degrees, health plans, and even our worship services. We want a church service on a convenient day at a convenient time with a style of music we enjoy and a sermon that does not exceed 15 minutes. We say worship is an important part of our lives, but we do not want to put any energy into it. Pastors may fall into a similar rut—experiencing worship as a weekly task with a list of objectives to accomplish by the time the bulletin goes to press.

We need to find a way to worship with our hearts, bodies, minds, and souls engaged. Living faithfully is working with and for a community of faith from a deep love of God that cannot be denied. Allow yourself to be moved by the Spirit, through music, the Word, works of art, and the power of a community of believers. Although there is comfort in the familiar, one risks being lulled into a rote practice of religion. Think about the words you are singing. Personalize the prayers. Sing from the heart. Appreciate the silence. Active worship can be compared to healthy physical activity. When physicians ask their patients about physical activity and the response is, "I'm active at work," we reply, "That doesn't count." Repetitive movement at work, although activity, is often more detrimental to health than helpful. Healthy activity involves the whole body, and is done recreationally outside in nature. Just as we need healthy physical activity, we need to experience meaningful worship regularly to maintain our spiritual health—joyful worship with inspiring music that touches the heart, meditation on God's word bathed in the light and the warmth of the sun's rays through stained glass, a soaring hopefulness felt with every baptism.

Be aware of these sacred moments. Recognize the sustenance we receive from rejoicing, meditating, and praying.

Just as we have different ways of maintaining our emotional health, having an active personal faith means being true to our own personality. Worship, praise, prayer, and meditation mean different things to different people. For introverts, these activities may be internalized—quiet and individualized, nearly imperceptible to the onlooker. Extroverts want to join others in raising voices in song and word. Some of us may express the Spirit's presence through movement or vocalizations, and others in complete silence. Some feel the power of prayer in groups—praying in unison and offering petitions. Others feel closest to God in the silent darkness of night, or by the light of a single candle. For pastors who continue to preach and lead ministry, personal worship may be in a few silent moments before the service begins. It may be in the inspiration that comes in preparation for sharing God's word. Or it may be in the sacraments or in the faces of the worshipers. It may be in the Sabbath practices that are not related to Sunday worship. Planning for a meaningful worship life is important for each one of us—whether we are congregational leaders or members, pastors or laity. Retirement is an important time to establish a meaningful active faith life—individually and in the context of congregation and community.

Rest and Renewal

Just as we all need to find a meaningful place of worship, we all need Sabbath time for our health and wellness—especially pastors, whose lives are not their own when needing to be responsive to the needs of others. We Americans worship busyness and productivity. As individuals, we work longer hours, try to produce more in less time, work around the clock, and schedule other activities around work. Consequently, evenings and weekends are filled with shopping, medical appointments, education events, and church meetings. Churches are not exempt from this productivity expectation—"successful" churches are often measured by their membership, the number of pastors or size of staff, the number of programs, and the annual budget. For the pastor and for the members, the church becomes another competitive place where reputation and appearance become more important than reflection and renewal.

Certainly God knows the value of rest, renewal, and reflection. The seventh day was created as a day of rest, a day when God could reflect on the "goodness" of creation. We have lost the concept of Sabbath. We feel the need to attend to work issues every day and to meet our family's needs in any remaining time. We need time for ourselves and for God and for reflection on what that relationship means in our life.

Many have written about Sabbath-keeping. It is not just a day of worship but a day for ceasing work, finding rest and renewal, appreciating the beauty of life, honoring relationships with God and with our family, experiencing God's love for us, and expressing our love in return. Busy weeks, full of important meetings, phone calls, e-mail messages, errands, or even parties, distract us from God's love. We take that love for granted, just as many of us take for granted food, clothing and shelter, clean air and water, rapid transportation and communication, and climate control. Making time for Sabbath in our daily lives is essential for spiritual health and wholeness. Contemplating retirement is another opportunity to assess the life we are now living and how we might want to make changes to improve our health and happiness.

I just returned from a speaking engagement with a group of retired pastors on retreat. It was a wonderful experience, sharing time and conversation with a group of men and women enjoying each other and celebrating their lives and God's love. This retreat was Sabbath time—a chance to reconnect with friends, enjoy the surrounding beauty of the mountains, learn something new, and experience the fellowship of believers. One picture I will never forget—the faces of each and every participant as the group sang "Jesus Loves Me." They glowed with an ageless joy. They sang with the unbridled enthusiasm of preschool children singing in front of the congregation. It was a pure moment of living faith expressed as a result of this special Sabbath time. They had sung other hymns, told stories, laughed at jokes, and shared their frailties, but this song was an expression of their absolute belief in those words: "Jesus loves me! This I know."

> Ellen knew that it was time to clear from her life path unnecessary distractions. She intentionally started again on a journey of personal faith discovery and growth. She found a spiritual director and started a spiritual journal. She created a special place in her home where she would begin and end her days in prayer and meditation. She arranged with her church board to focus her upcoming sabbatical on spiritual renewal. She read, studied, prayed, and wrote in her journal. She spent some time in silent retreat at a nearby monastery. She spent hours at the piano, playing and singing her favorite hymns. Every day brought her closer to God and to a greater sense of tranquility. As her sabbatical was coming to a close, Ellen began to get excited about returning to her ministry. She knew that this time, she needed to keep the path cleared for her lifelong spiritual journey by continuing the spiritual habits she had developed on sabbatical.
>
> For Ellen, Sabbath had been about worship, about preaching the Word and providing the sacraments to help others on their spiritual journey. On her sabbatical, she rediscovered the true meaning of Sabbath and understood that staying on a spiritual path was essential for personal rest and renewal. When she returned to her normal life at home and in public ministry, she continued to begin and end every day in prayer. She protected time for study and devotion.

She continued to write in her journal and to meet periodically with a spiritual director. She knew that continuing those Sabbath practices would continually refresh her for a more vibrant and thoughtful ministry. Rekindling her personal relationship with God and protecting the time for prayer and devotion gave her the energy and the clarity to be more effective in her ministry. During her sabbatical she had a conversation with her spiritual director about time management in ministry. She recognized that her time in ministry was God's time for God's faithful, but she also recognized that to make the most of her time in ministry, she needed her personal time with God.

Sabbath practices help to maintain spiritual health but are also directly related to physical health. One of my professors at Harvard Medical School was Herbert Benson, physician and researcher, who wrote about and studied the relaxation response.[9] I recently heard him lecture on the history of his work. For decades he studied the body's response to practiced relaxation by teaching individuals relaxation exercises and by studying individuals from many faiths who practiced prayerful meditation. One of the discoveries in this research was that the positive impact of chanting on the body was more significant if the words used had religious significance. The rhythmic repetition of deeply meaningful words creates a state of relaxation that has positive effects on physical health. Many of us, if asked, would say that we make a habit of daily prayer, but does that prayer bring us closer to God? As we pray, are the words meaningful to us, and are they an expression of that deep connection through the love of God? Or are they the rushed words of a rote memorized mealtime blessing or bedtime prayer? My daughter confessed, as a young adult, that when she was a child she thought we prayed in a foreign language. As we rushed through the children's bedtime ritual, we always prayed, "Now I lay me down to sleep. I pray the

Lord my soul to keep...." While these words were familiar, she wondered for years what "Fyshuddye" meant. Are we just mouthing words that have lost their meaning? Or are we in true conversation with God?

I hope that as adults we have not lost that childlike expectation that our prayers, spoken, whispered, or thought, are heard and answered by God. For spiritual health, we need the reassurance that God is listening to our daily needs and thoughts and is there to help us with the strength and wisdom to bring others to understand the love of God. Retirement is a time when conversation with God is especially important to help redirect energy and passion toward meaningful work and relationships.

Making It Real

Prayer as ritual can become pure recitation rather than meaningful conversation, an event rather than a relationship. In the same way, Scripture can be seen as meaningful stories, and good works can be regarded as part of the mission of a congregation. Living a faithful Christian life means living out the story of the gospel daily—in our work, family, or congregation. Joan Chittister, member and former prioress of the Benedictine Sisters of Erie, writes, "We read the Scriptures faithfully but fail to apply them. We listen to the needs of the poor but forget the reading of the gospel entirely. We go to spiritual directors regularly but ignore or overlook the insights of the people with whom we live. We prefer to hear ourselves than to listen to wiser hearts for fear they might call us beyond ourselves."[10] Our spiritual practice should not be saved for Sunday, bedtime, meals, or holidays. Every day in every way we need to walk in the Word, listen for Christ, and see the Holy Spirit at work in the world.

As Americans, we like to compartmentalize things. We have different roles, clothes, and relationships for work, home, and

church. Our experience in each of these places is essential to
defining who we are, and we do not typically relate one to the
other. We go to work and perform our role, relating to co-
workers and parishioners, clients or customers. We go home,
change clothes and relax—engaged in individual or family
activities or chores. Sunday is for church—with Sunday clothes
and Sunday folks. We believe we know best and that we do
not need to listen for the voice of God. We recognize and are
grateful for the efforts of others who are "holier" than we
are, those who shelter the homeless, welcome the refugees,
feed the hungry, or parent the unloved. Early in life we are
learning roles—student, parent, worker, professional. It takes
a lot of energy to be learning as we are living. Putting our life
in compartments makes things easier. As we mature in life
and master several roles, I hope we have less need to compartmentalize and more ability to be whole—an individual person
who has many roles and the potential to take on new roles.
We also begin to see that compartments are somewhat artifi-
cial—that we aren't different in different settings. In fact, integrity often demands that we begin to break down the walls
and move easily from one role to another. We no longer need
to keep those compartments separate, with cues to remind us
which compartment we are in. We feel the need for continuity
and meaningfulness in our daily lives. Retirement presents an
opportunity to bring different aspects of our life together, not
constrained by location, role, or calendar.

As adults with life experience, emotional maturity, and
spiritual grounding, we can read the gospel and make it real
in our daily lives. We have more time to feed the hungry and
to care for those who are homeless or unemployed. We can
work with others to address the injustices of Americans without health care or children without safe homes. We need to
forgive those who have sinned against us and reach out to
those who need love. Ministry and mission may take on new
meaning. Making the time for and developing the practices of

daily prayer, devotional meditation, joyful hymn-singing, meditational walks, or communing with each other and with God are essential for good health. The sense of peace, the warmth of shared love and faith, the appreciation of the immensity of the gifts received and the emotional cleansing of raising voice in song bring healing benefits that last throughout each day and week.

For Reflection

1. How do you live out your faith?
2. When and how do you find the time for rest, renewal and reflection? It may be daily, weekly, monthly, or annually. How do you protect that time?
3. Who is your spiritual mentor? Why?
4. Recall a story about living out the gospel in today's world. What does that experience mean in your life, and how can it be experienced again and retold?

8

For Those We Leave Behind
Dying Well

Our bodies, as miraculous as they are, were not designed to run forever, like the Energizer Bunny. Acting as if we were invincible may be a transient, adolescent phase. Investing in your health at every age is honoring the miraculous gift you were given by God. Accepting eventual death is a healthy response to the reality of our earthly bodies. Planning and preparing for that transition is important throughout life, but these tasks become even more important as we approach the end of our expected lifespan. In America, life expectancy for someone born today is 74 years for men and almost 80 years for women. Midlife is often the time when we first recognize that we are closer to the end of our lifespan than to the beginning. It is the first time we acknowledge that planning our lives is a finite rather than infinite process. As you read about ways you can prepare for a rich and meaningful retirement, think about what is most important when you know the end is near, and what is important for those you will leave behind.

American culture emphasizes living life to the fullest, with little thought of living with limitations, or of dying. We focus on reaching our highest potential—of beauty, strength, speed, position—and look for health only when we need a medical cure or a rescue from life-threatening disease or injury. The Evangelical Lutheran Church in America has written a social statement on health, healing, and health care. As an important reminder to the church about its role in health care, the report states, "We can always care, even when we cannot cure."[1] Hundreds of thousands of dollars are spent in the last months of life. Most people want to die in their homes and not in a hospital, and yet most Americans *do* die in the hospital. Western medicine is centered on cures—rescuing people from the brink of death, diagnosing disease with the most advanced technology, even erasing the signs of natural aging. Death is hidden, sanitized, and prettied up. Death is no longer a natural part of family life. Individuals on the brink of death have machines to breathe for them, medicine to keep their hearts beating, and intravenous nutrition. In many other cultures, families care for the dying at home and in hospitals and prepare the body after death. They don't use expensive technology; they use their loving hands and voices.

It is difficult for us to think realistically about our own death, when our culture avoids the intimate experience of personal death and the media bombard our senses with scenes of violent death in games, movies, and television. We are afraid of death because we are afraid of the unknown. We have no positive images to relieve our fears. How can we find peace or acceptance in isolated, sanitized, technology-driven final days? How can we have a realistic picture of the dying process, when the images we have are those of violence? How do we as family members know how to care for the dying and ease their transition when we have never witnessed death?

In this third age, as we think about retirement, we prefer to focus on the rich life we hope to enjoy for the next decade or two. But this is also the time to think about, or to reconsider, our plans surrounding our death. As a society and as individuals we have to accept that life comes to an end. While we can do our best to live healthy and whole lives, the time of our death is not known and cannot be postponed indefinitely. As individuals, each day we are one day closer to our death, and there is more urgency to be prepared. Any planning and preparation we do in advance brings us and our family members a sense of peace and brings us closer to accepting the inevitability of death. As a society and as a church, we need to help each other to prepare and support each other on our journey as we live our final days. As faithful Christians, we have the hope for everlasting life, the gift of the resurrection. That should allay our fears. It is this belief that should give us as a church the strength and the passion to accept the responsibility of teaching and helping others to die well.

Paul's light burned brightly—he was intense and unquenchable. He stood out from Day 1 as the seminary student to watch and emulate. His face glowed with the excitement of being at seminary. He was impatient from the start to be serving a congregation. He had work to do, and he was driven to get at it. He had been a church youth director and a Sunday school teacher. From age 12, he had known he would be a pastor. Every day was another day closer to that goal. His free time in college was spent on a gospel team, singing and telling the gospel story at every opportunity. That is where he met his wife, Julie. They were married in college, and she worked long hours when they were in seminary so that Paul would be able to concentrate fully on his classes.

His internship was in a growing parish in a college town. His enthusiasm and people skills were a good match for the congregation, and he got along well with his supervising pastor. He was comfortable in his role of public ministry but also humble and willing to learn from the pastor and parishioners. The year was wonderful for Paul and Julie, and it was no surprise to anyone that he returned to that parish for his first call.

After six years in his first congregation, Paul received a call to a challenging ministry. It was an urban congregation struggling financially and losing membership. It was hard to leave the many friends he and Julie had made in their community and in the congregation, but Paul knew it was the right decision. He rolled up his sleeves and called the leaders of the new congregation together, and they wrestled with the mission of their ministry and with the challenges of the community. The people grew to love them both, and the joy that emanated from the church became infectious. They started an after-school program and evening Bible classes. Membership stabilized and then began to grow. The congregation celebrated each baptism, including that of Paul and Julie's second child, as a symbol of the renewal of the life of their church.

Two years into this call, Paul began to experience headaches. He wrote them off to being busy. It wasn't unusual for him to skip lunch and sometimes dinner because of the demands of his church and community. Julie finally insisted that he see a doctor. After several weeks of continuing headaches despite several medications, Paul was found on the floor of his office one afternoon by the part-time church secretary. He was groggy and unable to tell her what was wrong. She called for an ambulance and then called Julie. The news from the emergency room was devastating. A CAT scan showed a large brain tumor. The news spread through the community in hours.

After consultation with several physicians, the news was no more encouraging. The tumor was inoperable because of its location. Chemotherapy was the only option and was expected to relieve symptoms but not to cure. Paul was able to return to ministry and seemed inexhaustible and unchanged, except for his hair loss. After several months, however, he began to tire easily. He reduced his hours, and the bishop's office was able to provide part-time help. Julie quit her job and stayed home to care for Paul and the children. Her mother lived nearby and was able to help also.

After a month of part-time work, Paul was no longer able to get to the church office. He asked Julie to help him work from home. She made a bedroom/office in the front room of their home where he would spend two hours in the morning meeting with his congregational leaders and members. He wanted to share with them his vision for the future of this congregation and to share time with those to whom he had become very close. These hours were precious to him but were strictly observed. He and Julie knew that, as important as his congregation and its ministry was to him, he had precious few days left to be with family.

His physicians had arranged for hospice care months earlier. The hospice nurse helped with managing medication and other therapies to relieve his symptoms and yet to keep his mind clear enough to spend quality time with loved ones. The hospice chaplain had worked with him to write a journal for Julie and their children, to share what was most meaningful to him, his precious memories, and his dreams for the future. The chaplain reminded him about the need to preserve time and energy for his own prayer and devotions. Paul's faith never wavered, but his personal prayer time was often interrupted by those who loved him. All who came to see Paul in those last weeks spoke of the light of life and love that shone in his eyes. Julie was grateful for the time they had to spend together and with the children. She knew that his life was full and that he was ready to die. They had finalized the details of funeral service and burial and were celebrating each day as it came. They sang hymns together, and when he was no longer able to sing, they played CDs quietly in the background.

We cannot know the details or the timing of our death. In chapter 7, you learned about the studies on clergy longevity. While earlier research showed that clergy lived longer than people in many other professions, more recent studies show clergy with increased risk for heart disease. We can, and should, work hard to improve our health and wellness. It is not longevity but rather quality of life that is the goal. Yet we must also plan and prepare for our death. If you have not already done so, now is a good time to draft advance directives and an ethical will. Attend to unfinished business and practice forgiveness. Speak of your love for family and for God. Let your family members know how you want to be cared for during the dying process, how you want to be remembered, how you want to be buried, and where. We may not know the timing, but living in wellness means being prepared for death.

Prepare for the Inevitable

Advance health directives are a gift to your family. A living will is a signed document that makes known your wishes about what kind of treatment you want when you are ill or injured and not expected to recover. Preparing directives also includes naming an agent with durable power of attorney for health care who will make decisions on your behalf if you are unable. When no preparation has been made, people react emotionally and without much thought about what you may have wanted or what might be best for you and for your family. Faced with a traumatic event—severe illness or injury—family members are devastated by emotions and unable to think clearly about difficult or complex questions. Having conversations with those closest to you in times of health and happiness begins to pave the way for making difficult decisions. Having some knowledge of your feelings and wishes about pain control, hospice, nursing homes, hospitals, resuscitation, and what is important and comforting to you—music, pictures, visitors, family presence, Bible verses, hymns—gives family and friends something positive to do that is invaluable in a situation that may feel out of control. Having written instructions that explain your wishes, along with an informed health agent, gives everyone a sense of peace and relieves the struggle that family members may have in making difficult decisions that may be inconsistent with your wishes.

Every state in the United States has specific rules about advance directives and specific forms to be filled out and witnessed or notarized. (For more information, log on to *www.uslivingwillregistry.com*.) Most include detailed questions with space for individualized responses. Completing this document is the first step in preparation. The next step is to discuss the information in the document with family or friends, particularly those designated to make decisions on your behalf. The document must be available to those who are responsible for making such decisions—your health-care agent and your physician(s). You can give copies to your physician, clinic, hospital, or all three. You can carry a copy with you in the car or when you travel. You can even get wallet cards or bracelets engraved with your decision about resuscitation or indicating where to find directives. There are Web sites where individuals can post their own directives that can be accessed as needed. These directives must also be updated as often as needed to address changes in health, health care services, or family situations.

Beyond selecting a health-care agent and completing and discussing an advance directive and living will, one might want to write an ethical will. Dr. Barry Baines, family physician and hospice medical director, has developed this concept as a guide to helping individuals leave behind a legacy for their family members.[2] Preparing an ethical will provides the opportunity to think about and write down your thoughts and feelings, life story, values, and dreams for the future as a gift to your family and friends. It is another step toward dying peacefully and dying well—in the knowledge that you are prepared physically and emotionally and that you have prepared those you love (see chapter 2).

Living in Wholeness

Being prepared for the inevitability of death frees us up to focus on life. Having a plan for dealing with the issues of dying and resolving as many as possible before death is near—

getting finances in order, dealing with emotions, discussing transfer of material goods, resolving legal issues, learning how treat symptoms and accept physical care—gives us more time and energy to be with those you we love, laughing out loud and doing the things that we enjoy.

We all know we are dying. Some know the time frame with more certainty than others. Sometimes death takes us and our loved ones by surprise. Others have days, weeks, or months of awareness that this life will end soon. Preparation for death and dying well has everything to do with balance in life. This balance includes maximizing physical energy, expressing and understanding emotions, learning about illness or the dying process, making time for family and friends, reflecting on vocation and life history, and making time for and deepening your relationship with God.

The Wholeness Wheel (see page 5) is a guide for this preparation. Just as it may be used as a prescription for health in daily living, it can be a guideline for preparation for dying well. In terms of physical wellness, planning may include making changes in your home for handicap accessibility or to plan for other living arrangements if the time comes when you are unable to take care of your daily needs in your home or current living situation. It certainly includes having a physician whom you trust to help manage your health, treat illness, or help to relieve suffering and work toward a peaceful death. It is a reminder that nutrition, sleep, and physical activities remain essential to preserving energy and maximizing health even in the context of illness.

Preparation enhances emotional health by relieving some of the fear and anxiety many of us experience when considering our own death. As we think and talk about issues that may surround our death, we may experience relief about not leaving others unprepared, and comfort from knowing that family and friends understand our wishes. Being able to think about and plan for our deaths includes some reflection on meaningful life experiences and results in a certain level of acceptance. Anticipating and resolving issues that may affect the family—whether financial, vocational, spiritual, or emotional—will relieve some of the anxiety about having unfinished business or leaving others with burdens, and may enable us to face death more directly. We have learned from those who have died or have suffered a near-death experience the importance of living each day in the knowledge that we are dying. Such individuals remind us of what is most important to our emotional health—saying "I love you" to all we love, seeking forgiveness, taking time for prayer and devotion. There is no time for sustaining anger or guilt. Having fun is not just a luxury to be reserved for vacation or Fridays. Laughing should be part of every day's experience.

As we discussed in the chapter on relational wellness, we do not do well in isolation. Given the importance of relationships for wholeness, it makes sense that people would fear dying alone. Continuing to nurture existing relationships and to build new relationships is important throughout life. Make time for your family and friends. Travel to see them, or invite them to your home. Be an active member in your congregation, participate in Bible studies, service activities, choir, or other small groups. Reach out to your neighbors and be active in your community. Spend special days with your grandchildren, nephews and nieces, or neighborhood children. Especially if you find yourself living alone, get a pet or make a ritual of a daily or periodic call to a friend or family member. We cannot control the moment of death. But it is good to remember that even if we are taken from life when we are alone, we are not truly alone if we have the love of others surrounding us and are certain of God's love.

While we may have retired from our occupation, we have vocations until the end. Sharing our gifts and talents and the love of God with others continues to give us a sense of purpose. We might carry out our vocation by telling stories to grandchildren, creating expressions of our love for each member of our family, drawing pictures to delight others, making others laugh, singing hymns or other songs, praying with others, or sharing in devotions. We may listen to and comfort others or give sage advice. We are here on this earth for a reason, and even when we don't have much energy, a simple word or look or gesture can be important at that moment and can also leave a lasting memory. Some authors have made the case that even a person in the last stages of dementia has a vocation—to receive the care of family, friends, and caregivers who are called to vocations as spouse, children, nieces and nephews, siblings, nurses, and nursing assistants.

> Paul died too young. His friends, family, and parishioners were shocked by his cancer. Some were angry, others very sad. Paul had his moments of disbelief and sadness after he heard the diagnosis, but he had lived his life for Christ, and he knew that was what he needed to continue to do. Each day was a new day and a gift from God. Whether it was a day for chemotherapy treatment or a day of play with his children, every morning he offered up his life to God as a vessel for God's love. Just as he had known at age 12 that God had a plan for him, he knew now that each day had a purpose, and he asked God for the clarity to know what was needed each day, the strength to accomplish what he could, and the wisdom to turn over to the care of God what he could not do himself.

Hospice Care Is for You and Your Family

Many of us have not been exposed to death or witnessed the moment of death. It can be a very special time and an opportunity to lessen our fears about our own death. Hospice care is a team-oriented approach that provides expert medical care, pain management, and support tailored to the needs and wishes of a dying person. Created out of a recognition that most of us are unfamiliar with death, hospice care addresses all dimensions of wellness for the patient who is living with a terminal diagnosis and for that patient's family. The object of those services is not to cure, but to help to meet the patient's physical, emotional, intellectual, social/interpersonal, vocational, and spiritual needs. This is done within the person's home environment or another environment designed to be homelike. The care of the patient is personalized. The care team recognizes who this person is, who she has been, what is and who is important to her.

The hospice caregivers are experts in the dying process and can be instrumental in teaching the patient, family, and sometimes the doctors about the realities and the needs of the dying. Hospice workers become very familiar with the patient and the family, often knowing what they need without being asked. They help to address the patient's needs as the patient wishes. For example, some people may want to control pain with medications, even if that means more drowsiness. Others are willing to tolerate some pain for the gift of being aware of the life around them. Hospice staff members have learned much about pain control and comfort measures, and their knowledge is being expanded to palliative care—care that eases symptoms of an illness and improves the quality of life for those who need that kind of care but do not anticipate death in the near future. Hospice workers will recognize stages of dying and help to prepare the family, contact the chaplain, pastor, or physician, and comfort family members and friends. One of the most frustrating experiences for those familiar with hospice care is to hear patients and family say they wish they had known about or accepted the services of hospice care sooner.

Many hospice services are covered by health plans and government payers, but check with your physician or the hospice providers to answer your questions. Hospice care is a gift to individuals and families as they face the challenges of the transition from this world to the next. Take the time to become familiar with the hospice services available in your area, tell others about these services, and think about volunteering your own time and services in the care of the dying.

Dying Peacefully

We fear death because it is unknown. Anxiety is lessened by preparation, by the services of hospice and palliative care experts, and by the love of those around us. But the fear of death is diminished most by trust in God and the knowledge that Christ died for our sins so that we might have salvation. We believe in the resurrection, which demonstrates God's ultimate power over death. Living in wholeness means living in relationship with God and believing in God's promise of everlasting life. It means being thankful to God for our life experiences and for each new day.

> Reunions are special events. They are events that may take months of planning and yet last only a few days. The impact of reunions is not limited to those few days, however. Reunions are occasions for reconnecting and sharing life stories. They reunite friends and acquaintances who shared a unique time and experience. I began this book with the story of a reunion of seminary classmates. Those formative seminary years shaped our vocations. We had great hopes and aspirations as students and seminary families. We were excited about the future and felt proud of our classmates. We needed to reconnect and share our life stories—to hear the details of the end of Paul's life, to hear about Michael's accomplishments and George's social ministry, to laugh with Jim and to listen to Jean and Ellen's transitions. Sharing our life stories validated our own struggles and experiences and inspired us to be attentive to our personal and vocational

life journeys. Each of us is now facing the prospect of retirement, in our own time and way. Sharing our pasts and contemplating our futures with friends who have led the way
healthfully is good preparation for retiring well. We are
thankful for friends and for faith in God, who shows us the
way.

For Reflection

1. Have you completed your advance directive, living will, and ethical will? With whom have you
   shared these?
2. What are your wishes and plans for your final
   days on earth?
3. What are your fears about dying?
4. How and with whom are you sharing your life
   stories?

Notes

Chapter 1: It's All about Change

1. Institute of Medicine, *Health and Behavior: The Interplay of Biological, Behavioral, and Societal Influences* (Washington: National Academy Press, 2001), 1-4.
2. Parker J. Palmer, *Let Your Life Speak: Listening for the Voice of Vocation* (San Francisco: Jossey-Bass, 2000).
3. Merriam-Webster's Online Dictionary, *www.merriam-webster.com*.

Chapter 2: Let's Get Real

1. Gwen W. Halaas, *Ministerial Health and Wellness Report 2002* (Chicago: Evangelical Lutheran Church in America, 2002).
2. William C. Knowler et al. "Reduction in the Incidence of Type 2 Diabetes with Lifestyle Intervention or Metformin," *New England Journal of Medicine 347* (2002): 1483-1492.
3. National Center for Health Statistics, *Health, United States, 2004, with Chartbook on Trends in the Health of Americans* (Hyattsville, Md., 2004), 159.
4. National Center for Disease Prevention and Health Promotion, *Chronic Disease Prevention Fact Sheet: Actual Causes of Death in the United States, 2000, www.cdc.gov/nccdphp/factsheets/death_causes2000_access.htm*.
5. Cynthia Stein and Graham A. Colditz, "The Epidemic of Obesity," *Journal of Clinical Endocrinological Metabolism*, 89 (2004): 2522-2525.
6. James O. Prochaska, John C. Norcross, and Carlo C. Diclemente, *Changing for Good: A Revolutionary Six-Stage Program for Overcoming Bad Habits and Moving Your Life Positively Forward* (New York: Avon Books, 1994).
7. Stephanie Paulsell, *Honoring the Body: Meditations on a Christian Practice* (San Francisco: Jossey-Bass, 2002), 79.

8. America on the Move, "The Partnership to Promote Healthy Eating and Active Living," *www.americaonthemove.org.*
9. Walter C. Willett, *Eat, Drink, and Be Healthy* (New York: Simon & Schuster, 2001).
10. Harvard School of Public Health, "Calcium and Milk," *www.hsph.harvard.edu/nutritionsource/calcium.html.*
11. U.S. Department of Health and Human Services, Public Health Service, Centers for Disease Control and Prevention, National Center for Chronic Disease Prevention and Health Promotion, Division of Nutrition and Physical Activity, *Promoting Physical Activity: A Guide for Community Action* (Champaign, Ill.: Human Kinetics, 1999), 5.
12. Maria A.F. Singh, "Exercise and Aging," *Clinics in Geriatric Medicine*, 2004, 20(2).
13. National Sleep Foundation, *www.sleepfoundation.org/sleeplibrary/index.php?secid=&id=57.*
14. Paulsell, *Honoring the Body,* 131.
15. Paulsell, *Honoring the Body,* 156–157.
16. H. Feldman et al., "Impotence and its medical and psychological correlates: results of the Massachusetts Male Aging Study," *Journal of Urology,*, 151 (1994): 54–61.
17. *AARP/Modern Maturity Sexuality Study* (Washington: AARP, 1999).

Chapter 3: Where's the Joy?

1. Terry Hershey, *Soul Gardening: Cultivating the Good Life* (Minneapolis: Augsburg Publishing, 2000), 21.
2. Daniel Goleman, "Emotional Intelligence: Issues in Paradigm Building" in C. Cherniss and Daniel Goleman, eds., *The Emotionally Intelligent Workplace* (San Francisco: Jossey-Bass, 2001), 13-26.
3. Institute of Medicine, *Health and Behavior,* 64-66.
4. Johann Christoph Arnold, *Seeking Peace: Notes and Conversations Along the Way* (Farmington, Pa.: Plough Publishing House, 1998), 231.
5. *Mental Health: A Report of the Surgeon General: Depression in Older Adults* (Rockville, Md.: U.S. Department of Health and Human Services, 1999).

6. Henri Nouwen, *The Inner Voice of Love: A Journey through Anguish to Freedom* (New York: Doubleday, 1996), 3.

Chapter 4: Use It or Lose It

1. American Music Therapy Association, *www.musictherapy.org/faqs.html.*
2. Interprovincial Board of Communication, Moravian Church in America, P.O. Box 1245, Bethlehem, PA 18016.
3. David Hirmes and Debbie Kaufman, producers, "3-D Brain Anatomy: The Secret Life of the Brain," *www.pbs.org/wnet/brain/3d/index.html.*
4. Monika Guttman, "The Aging Brain," *USC Health Magazine,* Spring 2001, *www.usc.edu/hsc/info/pr/hmm/01spring/brain.html.*
5. David Hirmes and Debbie Kaufman, "The Aging Brain. The Secret Life of the Brain," *www.pbs.org/wnet/brain/episode5.*
6. Webster's New World Dictionary and Thesaurus (New York: Macmillan, 1996).
7. National Institute on Aging, Alzheimer's Disease Education and Referral Center, *www.alzheimers.org/generalinfo.htm.*
8. Robert S. Wilson et al., "Cognitive activity and incident AD [Alzheimer's Disease] in a population-based sample of older persons," *Neurology,* 59, no. 12 (December 24, 2002).
9. David A. Loewenstein et al., "Cognitive Rehabilitation of Mildly Impaired Alzheimer's Disease Patients on Cholinestarase Inhibitors," *American Journal of Geriatric Psychiatry* (July/August 2004): 357-394.

Chapter 5: God Happens at Parties

1. Institute of Medicine, *Health and Behavior,* 4-8 to 4-9.
2. Harold G. Koenig, *Purpose and Power in Retirement: New Opportunities for Meaning and Significance* (Radnor, Pa.: Templeton Foundation Press, 2002), 94-95.
3. Barry K. Baines, "Writing an Ethical Will," *Minnesota Medicine* 67 (January 2004).

Chapter 6: Follow Your Passion

1. Institute of Medicine, *Health and Behavior,* 2-16.
2. Terry Hershey, *Soul Gardening,* 21.

Chapter 7: Faith and Life

1. Gary L. Harbaugh, *The Confident Christian: Seeing with the Eyes of Faith* (Minneapolis: Augsburg Fortress, 2000), 13-15, 150-158.
2. H. King and F. B. Locke, "American White Protestant Clergy as a Low-Risk Population for Mortality Research," *Journal of the National Cancer Institute* 65, no. 5 (1980): 1115-24.
3. Geoffrey M. Calvert, Jeffrey M. Merling, and Carol A. Burnett, "Ischemic heart disease mortality and occupation among 16-60-year-old males" in *Journal of Occupational and Environmental Medicine* 41, no. 11 (1999): 960-966.
4. Jeff Levin, *God, Faith, and Health: Exploring the Spirituality-Healing Connection* (New York: John Wiley & Sons, 2001).
5. Harold G. Koenig, *The Healing Power of Faith: Science Explores Medicine's Last Great Frontier* (New York: Simon & Schuster, 1999), 266-270.
6. Koenig, *The Healing Power of Faith,* 264-266.
7. Koenig, *The Healing Power of Faith,* 277-280.
8. Levin, *God, Faith, and Health,* 168-169.
9. Herbert Benson, *The Relaxation Response* (New York: HarperCollins, 1975).
10. Joan Chittister, *Wisdom Distilled from the Daily: Living the Rule of St. Benedict Today* (New York: HarperCollins, 1990), 15.

Chapter 8: For Those We Leave Behind

1. "Caring for Health: Our Shared Endeavor" (Chicago: Evangelical Lutheran Church in America, 2003), 15.
2. Barry K. Baines, "Writing an Ethical Will."